No One Is Too Far Away

Notes from a Transatlantic Friendship

Martin Baker and Fran Houston

Kingston Park Publishing

Published by Kingston Park Publishing, Newcastle upon Tyne, England

Published 2021.
First edition published 2018. Second edition 2021.

ISBN Print: 978-1-8383736-2-7
ISBN E-book: 978-1-8383736-3-4

Note: The authors write in their own distinct voices. In Fran's case this is American English. For Martin, it is British English. Spelling conventions have been preserved for each writer, with no attempt made to enforce consistency.

For friends near and far

Table of Contents

Introduction

Fran and I are best friends who live three thousand miles apart on opposite sides of the Atlantic. We met on social media in May 2011 and have been friends ever since. We've met once face-to-face, in June 2013, when Fran briefly visited the UK.

Fran lives with bipolar disorder, chronic fatigue syndrome, and fibromyalgia. Despite the distance, I am her primary support and caregiver. In our first book, *High Tide, Low Tide: The Caring Friend's Guide to Bipolar Disorder*, we share what we've learned about growing and maintaining a mutually supportive relationship, no matter where you are or how far apart you might be.

In this book, we present a collection of original articles published on our blog Gum on My Shoe between March 2014 and October 2018. We hope you find them interesting and informative.

As we like to say, no one is too far away to be cared for or to care.

Happy International Realness Day

Published March 20, 2014

TODAY IS THE first day of spring, International Happiness Day, and my birthday, so I guess I should be happy. As a matter of fact, I am, but the expectation that we should be happy on any particular day (our birthday, Christmas, a friend's wedding, International Happiness Day) denies our right to feel — and crucially to express — whatever we happen to be experiencing in the moment.

I tweeted earlier today that, for me, happiness isn't about being smiley and "happy happy" all the time. It's about being genuine and connecting with people. Maybe what I'm thinking of isn't "happiness" at all, because being genuine and connecting can and frequently does cover a wide gamut of emotions and experiences, not all of which are cosy or easy. Maybe it's "real-ness." It is what happens when we allow ourselves and each other to experience the moment, this moment, this today moment. Whatever you want to call it, it is what I find most valuable and rewarding in life.

Fran sometimes wonders why I'm always so pleased to see her, even when she is depressed or fatigued or otherwise "not good company." I prefer when she is stable and able to enjoy life, but the value and reward I find in our time together isn't dependent on her health or mood. It comes from us sharing whatever is happening in our lives openly and honestly as friends. And, of course, it cuts both ways. Occasionally (whisper it), it is me who is pissed off or angry or otherwise "not good company."

So, let's allow ourselves and each other to experience and share whatever we are feeling. I think we will all be a lot happier as a result.

[MB]

With Spots of Heaven Sprinkled In

Published April 10, 2014

IT'S HARD WHEN you have invisible, incurable, chronic illnesses. I have three. My days and nights are spent "managing" symptoms that come and go or linger, without any sense or reason. There is no control over the simplest of things. Conventional and alternative medicine has not substantially helped. For the past 20 years, I have tried everything. I have spent countless amounts of money.

Hope is running out. I work at acceptance but my patience wears thin. My courage is spent. The energy it takes to not complain — so I won't be judged or have endless "fixes" suggested by friends and strangers — is too much to bear.

I wish I had cancer. That would make things so much easier. It would be defined. It would be understood. It would even garner compassion. There would be an end. Either remission or death. With this, I live in a hell on earth with spots of heaven sprinkled in when I come up for air and a true friend grabs my hand.

[FH]

above ground, below ground

Published November 25, 2014

i am always amused when friends say wow you are out all the time doing lots of fun stuff..

truth is, the happy face on the outside doesn't always tell the pain, fatigue and torment on the inside.. photos posted from delightful places don't tell the story of what it costs to be there..

having three chronic invisible mental and physical illnesses is a full time job requiring much effort and care.. i rest a lot.. i meditate a lot.. i regularly flatline.. i work harder now than i ever did as an engineer..

time with friends, time with music, art, theatre, just time out.. is part of my wellness regime, as well as just something i like to do, as everyone does.. but it takes a lot to get there.. my bucket needs to be full or nearly full or i'll run into trouble..

self care, connections, and enjoyment are critical components of my staying alive..

only a few see the whole story.. i try to present well to the world, so others need not suffer my travails or worry about me.. and so I don't get hurt.. especially by well meaning ones..

what else is there but to smile anyway..

[FH]

will you?..

Published December 18, 2014

i'm doing really really well right now but it may not always be so.. i have bipolar.. it's not my fault.. it's not who I am.. i also have cfs and fibro.. will you still like me when i'm ill?.. will you ignore me?.. will you unfriend me?.. even block me?.. will you still love me when i'm not nice and sweet and how you'd like me to be?..

[FH]

Rewriting the Stories We Tell Ourselves

Published February 5, 2015

BE AWARE OF the stories we tell ourselves, especially those that begin "I'm not the kind of person who ..."

I'm not suggesting we ignore them all, some may still be valid. ("Marty, you're not the kind of person who attempts to go over Niagara Falls in a barrel." That one still works for me.) Most, though, are little more than strategies we've evolved to keep from expanding our horizons.

"Marty, you're not the sort of person who would do a charity zip-wire challenge from the Tyne Bridge."

"Marty, you're not the sort of person who strikes up conversations with strangers in coffee shops."

"Marty, you're so not the sort of person who writes a book about supporting someone with mental illness."

Well actually, it seems I *am* that sort of person, after all!

Let's listen to the stories we tell ourselves, and maybe we can rewrite a few of them.

[MB]

Let Stigma Go

Published May 29, 2015

HE SAID: Isn't she the one with the mental issues?..

He didn't say, isn't she the classical pianist?..
He didn't say, isn't she the one who loves Arabian horses?..
He didn't say, isn't she the talented electrical engineer, photographer, author?..

She replied: She is doing really well now.. She has a good heart and is a good soul..

I say.. Let stigma go..

[FH]

When I Am Depressed

Published June 7, 2015

WHEN I AM DEPRESSED, I am mean, edgy, negative, and argumentative. It is nothing personal. It is not even me. It is mental illness. My close friends know this and are full of support, understanding, and forgiveness.

It is a raging storm. We can only wait for it to pass and hope for limited damage.

At this time, I am completely unable to do simple tasks. Brushing my teeth is herculean. As is eating, cleaning, dressing. There is no floor.

And it feels eternal.

[FH]

Grace in the Midst of Chaos

Published June 9, 2015

LIKE ANY GOOD FRIENDS, Fran and I disagree from time to time. We crash heads and get grumpy with each other, but we neither run from nor ignore our issues. We are not afraid of them. We each acknowledge the other's point of view with respect. And then Fran gets her way!
//joke//

More generally, we recognize that disagreement needn't always be hurtful, nor is hurting something necessarily to be avoided. I find it unhelpful when people hold back from sharing with me for fear of hurting me, or do the big "sorry, sorry" thing if I share that I am feeling hurt or disturbed by what has arisen between us. Such responses invalidate my need to feel what is happening, and close down the space within which both of us might explore and grow.

As Fran messaged me earlier today, "disagreement can provide opportunity for growth and the stretching, openness and deepening of a relationship."

It is a beautiful thing ... the finding of grace in the midst of chaos.

[MB]

The World Hurts When One Leaves

Published June 17, 2015

BEAUTIFUL DAY.. Many folks out on the street and in the market.. I keep looking for those I know.. But they are not here.. They took their life.. All I can think is how could I have helped them stay.. How can we all help them stay.. The world hurts when one leaves.. I hurt..

[FH]

Kindness Is the Key

Published June 25, 2015

MARTY AND I met four years ago on a mutual friend's Facebook wall. She wanted to take her life. We didn't want to let her. She is still here today. I was headed toward the crest of mania at the time and wanted not only to save her but the whole world. That's how my friendship with Marty began. Even though Marty lives in the United Kingdom and I live in the US, he has become my best friend.

Four years ago, I was going through a hard time. I lived in a small community and my behavior led most people to assume that I must be drinking, that I'd stopped taking my meds, or perhaps I was just plain crazy. I've been told that everyone was worried about me at the time. However, apart from a very few, no one phoned to see how I was or came to visit. Mental illness is like that. No calls. No cards. No casseroles. I guess people were scared. So was I.

Marty was different. We chatted and emailed and did Skype calls daily (we still do). He didn't try to change me. He didn't try to fix me. He was simply there, listening, being a friend. He believed in me when I couldn't believe in myself. One thing he said was that he wouldn't go away no matter what I said or did. That enabled me to share freely with him. Without that safe container it's much harder to share with people because boundaries are unclear.

I started a non-profit to change the world. It was my Grand Manic Scheme. Marty helped me with it at first, until we realized it wasn't healthy. Then he helped me let it go. New meds, and my mania receded. I started to see the devastation and destruction I'd created while I was manic. A horrific shameful depression descended and engulfed me for the next eight months. Moment by moment thoughts of suicide pummeled me. Yet there was Marty, "holding my hand." There were times when I hated him for being there, for not giving up on me. He was patient. Gentle. Funny. He saw the spark for life inside me and kept fanning it, never asking me to change or be different than I was.

If it wasn't for him I wouldn't be alive. It's that simple. Our friendship is part of my wellness toolbox, as important as meds and other strategies I use to stay as well as possible. I take responsibility for my illness very seriously. Despite how it appeared to some people four years ago, I never missed an appointment or went off my meds at any time. They simply stopped working. That happens sometimes.

Social interactions can be lifesaving or death provoking. When people are aware and understanding they can be the tipping point between life and death. Kindness is the key.

[FH]

Be the Best Yourself You Can Be

Published September 12, 2015

Thoughts on World Suicide Prevention Day

I FEEL IT IS important to say that being there for someone who lives with suicidal thoughts and feelings isn't all about talking them down from a bridge or asking how many pills they took, what they were and how long ago.

In a crisis or intervention situation, yes. But for many people suicidal thoughts and feelings are an occasional or an ongoing reality and if we care for them we can support with the hope and intention of helping them keep from ever getting to the bridge parapet or downing the pills.

If you don't know how to approach your friend or colleague or family member, give it a go anyway. If you don't know what to say, say something, from a place of care and heart, not from a place of judgement or anger. Ask how you can help. Or just be quiet and be there.

Most of all, be yourself. The best yourself you can be. Because in that moment, your needs are not the issue. Your friend, your colleague, your family member, the person you just met, deserves nothing less.

[MB]

Got Tears

Published October 13, 2015

MANY YEARS AGO when my life completely fell apart, I cried like no one. I lost everything, outside and inside. The betrayal of my body took the cake. Every day for 2–3 hours for two years I wept. It was Niagra Falls weeping. And wailing. I played Melissa Etheridge while I was laid in my exquisite tub and let it all rip. I thought I would get to the end of it. That somehow if I cried enough my life would resume and get better somehow. Well no. I cried until there was not one more tear left. I gingerly picked up the broken pieces of my world and simply crawled baby steps. The only other option was death. I was close. I went to the woods of Maine. Where my eyes were like dried raisins. No matter if I was sad I could get no relief from tears no more. No relief at all. Today I have tears. Again. They squeak out like mice. And they are welcome.

[FH]

One Moment, Please

Published November 2, 2015

HAVE YOU EVER spent time thinking about all the things that support you? Or do you imagine yourself completely independent? I lay on my couch and began to wonder. I have a couch to lie on, rather than concrete. A window lets in light and beauty. Bookshelves hold books and lovely things. Walls are ever ready to be punctured for art and photographs. Plants offer me their oxygen freely. My fish gives joy.

Chairs invite sitting. Tables, dishes, glasses, silverware, napkins all cooperate to serve a meal. The fridge and freezer and cupboards endlessly receive and give food for nourishment. And let's not forget the pots and pans, the stove, sink, and dishwasher. Spices jockey for position, eager to delight our tongue. Smells tickle our nose. They all patiently await our attention. Do we listen? Candles wait to be lit. Lamps wait to be switched off. My bed beckons me into her womb.

Heat and cooling envelop me with no more effort on my part than the light press of a button. And the toilet flushes down my waste without a thought. Clothes hang in my closet, waiting to be worn. Shoes are ready to go walking. My shower gets the stink off and when I allow it, provides a spa experience. Towels gather me in their arms and as they gather the droplets, *poof* — I am dry.

Everything in your world serves you and teaches you to serve. Gratitude seems such a small word, when there is so very much to be thankful for. So the next time you struggle being thankful, take a moment to look around. [FH]

Spaceship Fran

Published December 4, 2015

I LIKEN MY body and mind to a spaceship. Not one all sleek and shiny and new and well-engineered. My spaceship looks like the hillbillies. Rusty and dented and old and engineered with duct tape. I need plenty of space to take off and land and navigate everything in between. My spaceship is rickety and noisy and overheats regularly.

It's a Herculean task even to hold onto the madly vibrating controls, let alone steer the thing. The windshield is foggy and pebbled. Sometimes friends help guide my ship when I am unable. They also help with maintenance, which also is often too big for me. Eternal thanks is my contribution.

The controls consist of lots of buttons and dials. When I push a button, I hope the something I want to happen does, but that's not always so. Sometimes things go on when I want them off and vice versa. Sometimes the dials get stuck, the screens freeze and crash, and I'm left relying on my instinct, which hopefully is not also defective.

It would be tempting to leave me in the corner of the junkyard, but even without all the strength and frills others easily enjoy, I still believe I am valuable. At least that part's not broken.

[FH]

Friends Fierce with Their Friendship

Published December 24, 2015

MY DEEP GRATITUDE for all those who never gave up on me during all my holiday-hating years. You all deserve jingles and bells and snowflakes and carols and pressies and happiness. When one has mental illness it's nearly impossible to feel anything but gloom or death or anger. Fortunately, I have friends who are fierce with their friendship. They see the tiny glow inside me and gently fan it. Because of them today I feel alive and strangely jolly and hopeful. May everyone have friends who let us stand on their feet without flinching and let us chance a look through their eyes to taste joy.

[FH]

Illness and Vulnerability

Published January 19, 2016

I HAVE LIVED with bipolar disorder, chronic fatigue syndrome, and fibromyalgia for more than 20 years. For a long time, I was full of rage, and sought any kind of fixing.

I went to the woods of Maine for a year to find my baseline. What I found was acceptance, within myself. My illnesses were no longer a problem.

Coming back into the world was much more difficult. I suffered stigma, rejection, and horrible ostracization, especially when I was in full blown mania and most needed help, despite precisely following doctors' orders and taking all steps for self-care. I would get so mad about people's misunderstanding me and what I was dealing with.

In time, I began to focus on the tiny bits that were good in my life, without expectation. Funny thing is, those tiny bits grew. Now, I have a small circle of diehard friends, and an ever widening circle of those who get it.

As Brené Brown says, "Don't try to win over the haters; you are not a jackass whisperer."

Thanks Brené!

[FH]

Living From Afar

Published February 5, 2016

I OFTEN HAVE TO live from afar. It may be that I am too fragile for company or live events. The overstimulation could be disastrous. It may be that I have been removed from a relationship or even a group. They may have deemed me unfit for social interaction because of behaviors and dialog exhibited during periods of mental illness. Or I simply said "no" one too many times.

Especially in these times I am grateful for technology and social media. Since I enjoy concerts, I make my own using YouTube, Pandora, Soundcloud. I meditate sometimes quietly, sometimes with music, sometimes guided. I also use YouTube to quiet intense insomnia. Facebook is a haven for staying alive. It's like Cheers. And you don't have to have a drink or even get out of bed. Skype keeps me tight with my best friend who lives on the other side of the world.

Yes, all these things can be addictive but only if you make them so. For me technology helps my heart grow.

[FH]

Nothing Left to Lose: Why I Write About Invisible Illness

Published February 13, 2016

THE REASON I write about invisible illness is because this is the biggest part of my world. The reason I share it on my social media, rather than only in my blog or in a closed group is because my biggest desire and fervent passion is for us all to talk about it out loud, upfront, in the mainstream. That is where it is spoken about least due to stigma and shame. Too many people have died from lack of talk, lack of connection, and lack of understanding. We who are ill have had to hide behind closed doors for way too long. Since I've lost everything short of my life I am no longer afraid. There is nothing left to lose but life itself. I am indeed a lucky one to still be alive.

[FH]

I lay under a tree

Published March 7, 2016

I LAY UNDER a tree. Not the biggest tree. Not the most beautiful tree. Not the best tree. Not the most comfortable tree. Not even a symmetric tree. I didn't even know what kind of tree it was. I paid attention to my inside world. I paid attention to my outside world. Until there was no difference.

[FH]

Who's Stupid?

Published April 10, 2016

THE THING ABOUT chronic illness is it never ends. It's not like you can be friends with someone and say nice things and then they feel better and get over it. Or tell them look at all the things to be thankful for, while they are tormented with symptoms.

Being friends with someone with chronic illness requires stamina, character, and a morality that is purely giving and compassionate, and yes even humorous.

The sooner society gets this message the sooner we can be a part of it, instead of separate from it. We have gifts, too.

But please show some respect. The last thing we are is stupid.

[FH]

How to Write a Status Report for Your Friend's Psychiatrist

Published April 11, 2016

SUPPORTING SOMEONE who lives with mental illness can be challenging, but there is a great deal you can do to help on a practical level, whether you live nearby or, as Fran and I do, on opposite sides of the globe. Something I am able to do for Fran on a regular basis is write a Status Report for her to take to appointments with her psychiatrist and care coordinator (case manager).

This helps Fran because she often finds it difficult to recall details, especially if she's been fatigued or depressed. She also values having another person's perspective. She sometimes asks other friends to offer their impressions of how well (or otherwise) she is doing, but I am best placed to provide an ongoing perspective, because we are in touch on a daily basis.

I welcome the opportunity to contribute to her care and support team. They value my input as someone who knows Fran well and can provide additional input. I prefer to write my report on the day of her appointment. I start from her current status, as I see it, but also refer back over the period (usually between two and four weeks) since her last appointment. There is no set structure, but I generally bullet point my comments and observations under the following headings.

What's Happening

A snapshot of what is going on for Fran at the time, listing any key events, successes, or concerns.

Physical Health

In this section I focus on Fran's levels of fatigue and pain, how she has been sleeping (insomnia can have a major effect on her other symptoms), and any other physical symptoms she has experienced recently.

Emotional Health

Fran's general emotional state, for example whether she has been feeling flat, irritated, frustrated, or angry; or positive, motivated, and engaged.

Mental Health

Here I note any red flag behaviors we have detected which might suggest she is slipping into either mania or depression; also whether suicidal thinking has been an issue recently.

People and Connections

Relationships are important to Fran, and a good indicator as to how she is doing generally. I list any significant positive or negative experiences she has had with friends or other people recently (whether locally or online), inviting Fran to explore these further during the appointment.

Anything Else

Anything that seems relevant which I have not mentioned elsewhere, including projects Fran might be working on, upcoming trips, or challenges.

[MB]

How Do You Respond to Challenge?

Published April 13, 2016

I HAD THE privilege this afternoon to listen to some inspirational speakers at a corporate event. The speakers included someone I respect highly as a colleague, and senior managers from across the globe.

The industry, sector, and account on which I work all face significant challenges in the months and years ahead, as many of us do in our personal lives. No amount of "happy happy talk" is going to make the issues go away, but that's not what was being offered today. It was a call to rethink our approaches. A call to engage in the workplace, in our wider community, most of all, within ourselves.

Returning to the office, I was saddened but not wholly surprised at the reactions I heard from other attendees to what, for me, had been an important and empowering message.

Cynicism, bitterness, resentment, and self-righteous entitlement are amongst the shields we habitually employ when challenged to think differently, and be more than we have imagined ourselves to be.

It doesn't have to be that way.

[MB]

The River

Published May 4, 2016

THERE ARE THOSE who are lucky. Their rivers have scarcely any stones. They live a life of luck and ease. Golden they are.

There are those who aren't. Their rivers rage and toss with leaks in their boat. They scream silently and sink to the rock bottom.

I live a river wild, a river free, for when the storms come my back leans into the wind, my front accepting, soft yet strong, my face gleaming with Mona Lisa smile, steady eyes seeing the prize, character arise.

[FH]

An Open Letter to My Bipolar Best Friend

Published May 15, 2016

Saturday, May 14, 2016

DEAR FRAN,

It is 11:30 a.m. here at Caffé Nero. 6:30 a.m. with you. My favorite corner table. My favorite time of the week. I've had something to eat and one coffee already. My second coffee (large black Americano, one extra shot) is close to hand. Normally I'd be looking forward to a call with you about now, but that will be late today because you have Laurel staying. We've chatted, though. In fact, I am chatting on and off with you on my phone as I write this letter!

I used to sit in coffee shops wishing I had someone to meet up with. Now, this place is my social hub. With friends online and friends face-to-face I meet and chat and share and talk and laugh here, regardless of geographic distance. What changed? You entered my life! In the five years since we became friends I have opened up enormously. Opened to you, opened into our friendship, but also opened to let others in, opened to let myself out. Our friendship has been and is transformative for both of us. This relationship between a well one (me) and an ill one (you) has turned both our lives inside out, and its impact ripples out into the world.

Yesterday I was severely frustrated because I couldn't find a way into writing the guest post I'd been invited to write for Men Tell Health. I had a few ideas, but nothing wanted to flow. You said I was jealous of the daily pieces you have been writing and posting for Mental Health Month. Not jealous — that would be to take away from your achievement — but envious, yes. You have such a gift for expressing what it means to live with illness, and I am proud to help edit and present your words to the world. My own writing comes much more slowly. I am a better editor than I am a writer, I think. I find it hard to "just write." I am my own worst critic!

You messaged me overnight: "Wish you were feeling less flat.. You wrote a book.. A whole fucking book.. Don't you give yourself credit for that?"

That jolted me out of my self-pity (thank you!) And you're right! I (we) have indeed written a whole fucking book! Our book, our story. A guide to inspire and inform others who, like me, support and care for a friend with mental illness. That's part of what I meant about our friendship rippling out into the world.

I got talking here at the cafe earlier with a guy who told me about a local writers' group — Newcastle Literary Salon — which meets once a month. I looked them up and the next two meetings are on mental and physical illness. I will go along, and see if I can get a slot to read from our book. It's scary to put myself out there in person, but that is part of what I've learned: to dare, to challenge myself whether it's doing a zip-wire slide from the Tyne Bridge to raise funds for Crisis, addressing the Mental Health First Aid team at Virgin Money, volunteering at the Time to Change Mental Health Day event, or appearing live on radio! I would never have done any of this if it were not for our friendship. Connection and challenge have become my watchwords.

When I was discussing my blogging "stuckness" earlier with Mike, he suggested I could interview someone for Mental Health Month.

"I'll make it easy for you," he said. "You can interview me!"

That says a great deal, I think, about the health of our father/son relationship. I am looking forward to seeing what comes of it!

The courses I've taken and the events I've attended have also brought me new people — my dear friend Claire who I met on the ASIST course. Darren who I first met at a Time to Change event, and who models for me a deep awareness of the human condition, respect and empathy for those struggling. Carol (via the radio show). Gemma (Mental Health Day). Angela (Time to Change). The list goes on and on! Online too, of course. We have made some amazing connections, both individually and jointly. Our friendship resonates with so many. Just by being ourselves, by being open and honest about what it's like to be friends when one friend lives with illness, by sharing our story, we offer something that — sadly — is not commonplace.

I am proud of us, Fran. Proud of what we do and are. Most of all, I am proud to stand at your side. I am proud to be your friend.

Marty

[MB]

I Was Going to Write Today

Published May 21, 2016

I WAS GOING to write today, but I didn't have my special pen with me.

I was going to write today, but my favorite table at the café was taken.

I was going to write today, but I was interrupted by my friend messaging me.

I was going to write today, but I was busy searching online for the perfect journal to write in because these things are important to a writer.

I was going to write today, but I wasn't sure anyone would be interested in what I had to say.

I was going to write today, but I was scared I would upset someone.

I was going to write today, but I was scared I wouldn't upset anyone.

I was going to write today, but the moment wasn't right.

I was going to write today, but my idea seemed too trivial to bother with.

I was going to write today, but my idea seemed too huge to get my head and words around.

I was going to write today, but whatever.

I was going to write today, but I had to go get groceries.

I was going to write today, but I couldn't find my brave.

I was going to write today, but there's always tomorrow, right?

I was going to write today, but I didn't bring my laptop with me.

I was going to write today, but they'll hate it.

I was going to write today, but they'll hate me.

I was going to write today, but I'm scared to discover who I am.

I was going to write today, but I'm scared to discover there's nothing there.

I was going to write today, but it's getting late.

And in the meantime, the world goes on. And other people write. And they are not necessarily "inspired." And they probably don't have the right pen or the perfect notebook. Maybe they found the back of an envelope to scribble on when their laptop crashed so they didn't lose what was bursting to get out. And maybe the cat just spewed up or the baby did. Or they feel sick today or depressed or despair of ever making a difference or even getting through another day fuck even another hour but you know what they dare anyway they dare to care and write and scream sigh vomit breathe craft something from the guts of them because sometimes that's all you have and all you can offer to the world and sometimes it is enough you are enough YOU ARE ENOUGH.

I was going to write today. Maybe I did.

[MB]

We Haven't Sunk Yet: Caring for My Bipolar Best Friend at Home and Abroad

Published June 6, 2016

THREE YEARS AGO this week, Fran was on board the RMS *Queen Mary 2*, en route from New York to Hamburg via Southampton. It was the start of a three-month European tour that we knew would seriously challenge her mental and physical health, and our friendship.

I tracked the ship's position and on-board webcam several times a day. With each hour that passed, my best friend was closing the 3,000 miles that had separated us since we first met online two years before. We were excited at the prospect of meeting face-to-face in Southampton, but we had never been as out of touch as we were through this week of the crossing.

On-board internet was prohibitively expensive, so our usual instant messaging, voice, and video calls were out of the question. We had arranged that I would send Fran a single text message each morning and evening, so she did not feel alone and isolated from the outside world, but it was too costly for her to reply. The week at sea was a lesson in trust and a powerful counter to co-dependency in our relationship.

In some ways, it was probably easier for Fran than for me. She was at the start of her adventure, acclimating both to the cruise and to the experience of being on vacation with her parents for the first time in many years. We'd had only four weeks to prepare, almost every moment of which had been focused on preparations, packing, and planning. We were both uncertain about the months ahead, but for now, she was aboard one of the world's great cruise liners, with staff on hand to take the strain, good food, and space to herself.

Fran loves to travel when her health and circumstances allow. In contrast, I am an armchair adventurer, more than content to be her virtual travel buddy when she's away from home. I'd accompanied her on trips to Spain, Panama, and Costa Rica — but we had always contrived to stay in touch. This was different, and I found it hard.

One dear friend helped me when I was starting to stress about it. She reminded me that when someone struggles with self-management the way Fran does, it can be a powerful thing to allow them to handle things in their own way. Fran knew I was there. My simply being there provided a sense of stability as she set sail (literally) from the routines and support systems of home. She needed me to be there, and to allow her to be where she was. That insight was a gift to us both. It reassured me in my role as Fran's support and caregiver, and also freed me to be myself. We would meet in just a few days, when the *Queen Mary 2* berthed in Southampton. For the time being, that was enough. I received one text message from Fran, halfway through the voyage. It read:

> We're over the midpoint.. It's very hard to sleep.. I've been walking and cycling daily.. Eating more than I should.. It's delicious.. It's a lot of fun.. Hi to everyone.. We haven't sunk yet..

[MB]

I Don't Take Vacations Away from My Friends

Published July 5, 2016

I'VE NEVER BEEN one to cut myself off from my "normal" life when I am on vacation. I know people who turn off their mobile phones and put their emails and social media on hold when they are away. It's not a matter of right or wrong, but that's never worked for me.

Connection is important to me and I'd feel I was denying myself something enriching and valuable if I were to turn my back on it all. As I like to say, I don't take vacations away from my friends; I take them with me!

I've always loved photography, and with my smartphone and a decent internet connection (a prime consideration when I am looking for new holiday destinations and accommodation) I can share my experiences more or less in real time, instead of having to wait until I return home to process and post my photos.

It's also important to me that I keep in touch with friends, especially those reciprocal relationships which benefit both parties and which have established regular, often daily or near daily, rhythms. Email, instant messaging, and social media allow the flow of energy to continue, enriched by the different perspective that comes from new places, people, experiences away from home.

It is especially important to me to maintain contact with Fran. She does not have the liberty of taking a vacation away from her bipolar disorder, her chronic fatigue syndrome, and fibromyalgia; nor is she able to put them on hold while I take a holiday. Being Fran's best friend, primary support, and caregiver is not onerous, nor is it ever a chore. But it is a role and a responsibility I take seriously. When either of us travels it disturbs our normal rhythm of connection and support, but we both work hard to maintain frequent contact in whatever ways present themselves. That is as true on a short break as it is for a week away — or as it was during 2013 when Fran spent three months travelling in Europe with her parents.

Right now, I am in the middle of a week's vacation in the English Lake District with my wife Pam. We ate breakfast this morning at the cottage we are renting, and then drove out for the day to Keswick. From past experience I knew I'd have an adequate data signal on my phone and found a lovely coffee bar in the centre of Keswick to take my midday Skype call with Fran (seven in the morning for her, on the east coast of the United States).

We spoke last night, and I knew Fran was struggling with fatigue and pain, depression, and some suicidal thinking in there for good measure. We talked at midday for 15 minutes (about average for our first call of the day) and I left her to sleep/rest before a morning appointment with her Care Coordinator. As I do for Fran's regular appointments, I'd emailed her a short "status report" — a bullet point listing of her mental, physical, and emotional standing as I saw it — early this morning before heading out.

It is now 6:40 p.m. and I'm hoping to connect with her again this evening to see how her appointment went. She messaged me to say it had been good, but it helps me gauge how she's doing if we are able to talk. It is also valuable for Fran herself. The regular nature of our calls is itself stabilizing, no matter what we get to talk about or do together. On top of all that, we enjoy each other's company!

I'm looking forward to sharing with her the great time Pam and I had in Keswick today. I have posted photos to my social media already but, as they say, it's good to talk. That's how friendship works for us.

No matter what is going on for me and Fran, health-wise or otherwise, we are friends first and last. I neither want nor need to put that on hold when I take a vacation, and the same goes for my other key relationships. At home or abroad, it's good to share!

[MB]

Work Work Work

Published July 19, 2016

STRESSING, STRIVING, and straining never got me anywhere but sick. I was totally committed to my goals and achieving them at all costs. And I did. I was very successful as an electrical engineer, loved my work. I had the car, the house, the mate, the life. However, I had no balance, no boundaries, which basically translates into no wisdom. Inevitably, coupled with sickness, I lost it all. After many years of thrashing and grieving, beauty appeared. I found that tiny bit inside that was true. I listened to that and it grew.

The same philosophy of striving can be applied to healing. Getting fixed, getting normal, getting free of whatever ails you. At all costs. There are a lot of people who are not shy to tell you what to do. I listened and clung to every word until I hit the wall with no money and no cure and was once again only left with that tiny little bit. This time I accepted my illnesses, even embracing them. I now saw them as teachers who were merely showing me how to care for myself and to rely on the wisdom within. Living from the inside out rather than forcing my lovely spirit into an external mold of ego. Trusting in that process is not easy but it is transformative.

We even strive with playtime. We operate under FOMO (fear of missing out) rather than JOMO (joy of missing out). I live in a beautiful place with abundant things to do, see, and eat. It has been a very long road to let go of having to do everything. And seeing everybody. And eating everything. My illnesses help guide me to choose, where my noes are, where my yeses are, and the stuff in between. If it's not at least 51 percent, it is definitely not happening. I've learned to choose that which is rooted in my higher values and freely and thankfully let go of the rest.

We are Americans. We are about work, play, success, the American Dream. Yet when we fall short of that expectation we get really silent. We feel like failures. We want to hide. The bigger truth is that we are human, and we are beings. What is inside of us is more precious than anything outside of us, no matter what money can buy. When I realized that, I became free.

Letting go of preconceived ideas of work, play, healing, and just about anything allows room for them to evolve and blossom from an original and creative space.

[FH]

The Meaning of My Name and My Aspiration

Published July 29, 2016

I DID SOMETHING remarkable yesterday. I laid down on a bed of tall grass in a graveyard. I gazed up at the sun sparkling through the trees. I closed my eyes. When my time comes, I won't be resting in the earth. I will be riding on the waves of the sea with my beloved Bo, a golden, an angel.

Friends may carve a stone or have a memorial. I only care that there is joy. I only care that there is kindness. I only care that there is freedom, the meaning of my name and my aspiration.

[FH]

Mental Health Awareness: It's Everybody's Business

Published October 9, 2016

LAST WEEK I was honored to participate as a speaker in the annual "It Takes A Community" forum organized by Maine Behavioral Healthcare. This year's theme was social media and mental health. It's a topic close to my heart. My best friend, Fran Houston, and I live 3,000 miles apart and have recently published a book sharing our experience using social medial and the internet to grow a strong, mutually supportive friendship between, in Fran's words, a "well one" and an "ill one."

Amongst other topics, the panel discussed people using social media to share their lived experience, whether as part of their personal response to illness, to help others living with similar conditions, or to participate in the wider movement challenging mental health stigma and discrimination.

Many, Fran included, share openly. Others are quite frankly too busy getting through one day to the next. Many have learned the hard way what it costs to raise their heads above the parapet. Or maybe they feel it is not their responsibility to enlighten a world that seems determined to misunderstand, misrepresent, and mistreat them. I agree it is neither realistic nor fair for society to expect those living with illness to challenge stigma alone, as I expressed in my closing remarks to the ITAC forum:

It isn't just about sharing the stories of those who have mental illness or are living with that themselves. It's about the families, the friends, all the rest of us sharing our stories of what that means to us and those who are dealing with this stuff. Because in terms of countering stigma it's not the responsibility of those living with mental illness to convert the rest of us. We are all in this together. It takes a community. We've all got to step up to this.

Yesterday, my wife Pam and I arrived at our holiday cottage in the English Lake District. Talking with Pauline, the lady who owns the cottage, the conversation turned to the book Fran and I have recently published. Pauline was very interested, and there followed a genuine and open conversation during which Pam shared her own experience — described in the book — with stigma and discrimination. This is what it takes. Connection. Conversation. Courage. The courage to say: "This is how it is for me." To ask: "How is it for you? How do you feel, hearing my story?"

Why does all this matter? Because mental illness is hard enough to live with, day in and day out, without society (which is to say, you and me) piling stigma and discrimination on top. Because people die from that. Because one in four or five (depending on how it is measured) live with mental illness. That means one in four or five of your family (yes, really). Your friends. Your workmates or classmates. Your congregation. Your fellow commuters. There is no us and them. There is only us. Be part of the conversation. Make a difference.

[MB]

Now I Know How

Published December 25, 2016

IT'S SURPRISING to find myself in the spirit of celebration. I'm rarely one for special days. Often I am depressed and grumpy, a Grinch, and having to fake cheeriness for others. A few years ago I began to look for little bits that light me up and dwell on them. There is so much excess and extravagance that can be overwhelming. My little bit grew every year. This year my table was graced with a garland, not one but two nutcrackers marched into my world, and an amaryllis bloomed magnificently by my window. These bits help me feel less alone. Next year a snow globe will sail on in. I never allowed myself to enjoy these frivolities before. But now I know how to cultivate a bit of joy and share it with dear friends, of course.

[FH]

One Day in the Life of Marty

Published December 28, 2016

Wednesday December 28, 2016

I WAKE AT 6:45 a.m., half an hour before my alarm goes off. I am always glad when that happens, I enjoy that "Ahhh, good, don't have to get up just yet!" feeling! I check my phone for any messages, snooze a little longer. I turn the alarm off with one minute to go. Rise, wash, dress, and am out of the house by 7:35.

As I walk to the Metro station, I message Fran "Good morning" for when she wakes later, and send a photo of the tree and path just outside our court. This is a new tradition, started a couple of months ago when the leaves on that tree were first turning towards autumn. It's a nice way of sharing how the weather is here in Newcastle without getting all meteorological.

By the time I've reached the Metro station, I've sent "Good morning" messages to two other friends, and a meds reminder to one. Not everyone would appreciate a daily reminder to take their medication, and I would never assume to do so without an invitation. It is a measure of trust on both sides, and not something to be taken lightly.

One friend surprises me by responding almost immediately. She is on UK time like me, but she's not back to work until next week so I wasn't expecting her to be awake yet. We chat as I catch my first train, then my second, and on my twenty minute walk. I share photos with her along the way. We have been friends for a couple of years. Mostly we chat when we are each traveling into work. I have come to enjoy her company on my commute.

I stop for coffee and a toasted cheese and egg sandwich at Quiznos, across the road from the office. It is just after nine o'clock as I arrive at my desk.

The morning passes easily. The days between Christmas and New Year are mostly quiet at work, and I make it through to lunchtime without anything major to deal with: a blessing as I am the only one in for my team this week. I'd normally expect a Skype call from Fran around midday (her 7 a.m.), but not today. I hope that means she is sleeping deeply. We will catch up later.

I check in on my social media accounts: mostly Facebook and Twitter, though I also love Instagram and Pinterest. Google Plus is still a mystery to me, and I make a note to apply myself to exploring it more in the weeks and months ahead. Maybe I can find an online tutorial.

The other friend I good-morninged this morning messages me to say hi, and asks how my day is going. We chat a little as she gets ready for her day. Like Fran, she is in the States, and her day is just beginning.

Social media is full of the recent deaths of Carrie Fisher and George Michael. As someone who habitually shies from mass emotional responses of any kind (be they nationalistic, political, sporting or whatever) I hold myself open to the various and varied tributes and resonances being shared online. The idea that this year — 2016 — has been "taking" the talented does not sit easily with me. I don't see things that way. But many do, and instead of closing myself down I can choose to be curious. To read and listen. So we learn.

A minor difference of opinion on Facebook yesterday led the other person involved to respond:

Your agreeable comment to my disagreeable comment [warmed my heart], a fellow human who respects different opinions and can discuss and laugh.

This is why I so value social media and the connections it brings. Another perfect example happens over my lunchbreak. I am on Twitter and connect with someone who runs an online training organization with her brother. We chat back and forth a little and she invites me and Fran to do a live interview with them sometime in the New Year. We friend on Facebook, LinkedIn, and Instagram. I love the Internet!

Around half two, Fran beeps in. She didn't have a good night's sleep at all. She has caught up on my news, via the "breadcrumb" messages I left her through the morning.

07:29: [Photo of the tree] Good morning! Frosty start to the day here

07:46: [Photo from the train]

08:31: [Photo from Quiznos where I had breakfast]

09:10: [Photo from the 3rd floor at work, showing the view across the park]

12:48: The morning has gone by quite nicely. Went across the road for a sarnie for lunch. The day is beautiful — still chilly but bright — the air feels clean and clear.

13:30: Have fixed us up with a live (Skype) interview sometime, with a lady who runs an online training organization here in the UK. Connected via Twitter. Don't worry I am not committing us to anything specific. She is going to email a schedule of when their slots are so we can talk about it and decide when (if we want to, though it seems a good match). We can talk about it later!

14:05: I have been doing a "day in the life of" blog. I will continue adding to it through today and post it up tonight or maybe tomorrow. It's not "amazing" — but I need to get over needing things I write to be "amazing" / "world-changing" all the time.

As I continue with my afternoon, Fran shares her weight with me. It has plateaued for a while now, though today it is up a bit. We have tracked our respective weights every day for the past three or four years. Over that time, we've seen how our bodies respond (and often fail to respond) to our efforts to achieve and maintain healthy weights. In Fran's case this is compounded by the effects of her medication. It is hard work to stick with a healthy regime, when the results do not seem to materialize.

Fran: I'm tired of exercising so much and doing well on my eating and drinking and having zero results. Makes me want to give up.

Martin: Yeah, but you know how that goes. Your weight goes UP fast and bigtime. Thing is to realign your definition of success. You are preventing your weight increasing. That is not "zero results," though it is not the result you are measuring against. (You get to hate me about now for saying that, it's okay!)

Fran: I know that but what the hell do I need to do to lose this goddamn fat? Starve?

Martin: Well not starve, no. I don't have your calorie history with me (it is on the big spreadsheet at home) but I know you have been keeping your weekly average calories down. You have done some particularly low calorie days recently, so I guess continue to do those kind of days in between the others.

3 p.m. and most of my colleagues have left (they started work before I did this morning). As I work, I keep an eye on my social media notifications. Friends sharing what they are doing. Friends sharing what they are feeling (or not feeling). What they are going through. It is not always pretty. It is not always easy. It is not always nice for me, but how much worse for these people I know and care about.

I have a reputation for being, in Fran's words, "pathologically positive." (It's not meant as a compliment.) Positivity in the face of hardship, one's own or another's, can be a defense mechanism. A shield. A way of running away. I did that most of my life. I still mess up. Hell, I fuck up. On a regular basis. But I am determined not to run away any longer.

Fran is heading out to the YMCA for her exercise class. I have another hour or so here in the office before home time.

It is now 9 p.m. Fran and I met on Skype between 7 and 8. We caught up on events and discussed our respective plans for the rest of the day. Since we ended our call I've drafted an email, and checked in on a couple of friends. Right now, my wife, Pam, and I are watching *Jonathon Creek* on TV. Fran and I will meet up again later, to discuss the interview with the online training organization I connected with earlier, and maybe watch an episode of our favorite show, the *Gilmore Girls*.

All in all, a good day.

[MB]

What My Mantra Means to Me: Healthy Boundaries

Published January 4, 2017

IN A RECENT POST I mentioned the mantra I've employed for the past couple of years, and chosen to carry forward into the coming year.

> Well-boundaried.
> Well-focused.
> Well-challenged.
> Well-loved.

But what does it mean? The resonances have changed over the past two years, and will likely continue to change. But what does my mantra mean to me right now? Of the four statements, "well-boundaried" is perhaps the least obvious, and I will devote this post to exploring its relevance.

I don't think I had ever heard of the word "boundary" in a psychological context before meeting Fran in May 2011. I can't recall precisely when or how it came up: most likely from us discussing the various therapies Fran had undergone or was undergoing. Or perhaps one of the online meditation classes we took together.

However it entered my vocabulary, it took a long time for me to see the concept of boundaries as healthy. To me, it implied an unhealthy erecting of barriers between me and the world, at a time in my life when I was learning to open up. It suggested precisely the restrictive concepts and practices I had been dismantling over the previous couple of years: in particular, the "Inner Circle vs. Rest of the World" model I'd employed most of my adult life.

My Inner Circle model had kept those closest to me within a high wall of my own devising. Inside, I felt safe, but it kept me from apprehending the World Outside or acknowledging those who dwelt there as more than part of the scenery. Policing the walls was exhausting, and one day I realized almost none of my Inner Circle still resided there. My Walled City had become a ghost town.

My response was to dismantle the city; take down the walls; dissolve the Circle. Like Titus Groan in Peake's fantasy series, I left Gormenghast and set out into the Wide World. It was scary, yet intoxicating. I was open to every new experience; each new encounter. I forged new connections; found new friends including, in time, Fran. I had found my new world view, unfettered by artificial boundaries and boxes. I had swapped the Walled City for the Wilderness.

Three books which I read or re-read around this time echo the transition. Robert M. Pirsig's *Zen and the Art of Motorcycle Maintenance,* which I first read at university, with its road trip Chautauquas and its blend of scientific and philosophic/metaphysical world views. A gift from a friend, *The Snow Leopard* by Peter Matthiessen expressed most clearly and cleanly for me the shedding of modern boundaries, as the author leaves behind his city existence to trek in the Himalayas. Henry David Thoreau's *The Maine Woods* also spoke to me of Nature and Wilderness: a particular American Wilderness, immersing me in the geography and history of Maine, and giving me insight into Fran's own wilderness experience.

I finally went to the backwoods of Maine for a
year and lived in a camp on 189 acres with no
running water and no electricity — an attempt
to find my baseline, fight my demons and find
the night, or die.

Fran Houston, "Lessons of the Night"

I began to see things were not so simple, and that a
completely un-boundaried existence was not merely
unhealthy but dangerous. This was something I was
learning first-hand with Fran. It had always been — and
remains — a fundamental of our friendship that I will
never ignore a call from her; be that by email, instant
message, text, or phone call. Day or night. 24/7/365. With
very few exceptions — and always by prior arrangement
— if her call comes through I will pick up.

However, I learned it's okay, indeed it's healthy, for
my response sometimes to be "Can't chat right now. I'll
get back to you." At times, I am busy and cannot be
disturbed: in a meeting at work, for example, with
someone else, or simply meeting my own need for space.
Recognizing our boundaries means Fran need never
worry she is going to upset or disturb me: if she wants or
needs me she can reach out knowing I will not ignore her.
But she also knows I will take responsibility for managing
my end of things. Fran handles her end on the same basis.
It is simple, it is healthy, and it works.

For me, boundaries relate most often to how, where,
and with whom I spend my time and energy. This was
very much the case when Fran and I were writing our
book. It took four years to bring *High Tide, Low Tide* to
publication, but it would have taken a lot longer had I not

defined and protected my "writing time." This mostly fell between 8 and 10 p.m., after my Skype call with Fran and before I settled to write my diary for the day.

The boundaries were not rigid: many times I chose to set them aside in order to spend time with friends, or because of other commitments. But it was important for me to have defined the boundaries and to feel justified in enforcing them when necessary. This did not (and does not) come easy to me. It is very much a work in progress, which is why I place it first in my personal mantra.

"Well-boundaried" also applies to my personal relationships. For many years, I held tightly to each and every close personal relationship (or, rather, to what they represented for me), in many cases long after the relationship itself had changed beyond recognition or faded altogether. In the same way I kept my "Special People" safe in the Walled City, I kept my relationships frozen; preserved; mummified. That is no way to honor anyone. When I left the City and set out on my grand wilderness adventure, I left the effigies of dead relationships behind me. (An echo here of Lady Cora and Lady Clarice, abandoned to die in their chamber within Gormenghast Castle.) Relics were no longer any use to me. I wanted living exchanges. I wanted dynamic relationships.

This meant setting aside lists and categories. It meant not labelling people ("Special People," "Friends," "Colleagues," "Neighbors" etc.), and opening my heart to experiencing people for who they are, and my relationships for whatever they might be in the moment. It meant letting go of prior expectations of what a "friendship" (for example) should or needed to be.

Not all relationships are healthy, however. I have had to acknowledge the concept of toxic relationships: not as a label of judgement or blame, but as a valuable descriptor. This has been hard, not least because I have far more examples of me being toxic to others than of others being toxic to me.

I find I have dismantled the rigidly boundaried Walled City only to discover — over there, in the distance — a region labelled "Do Not Enter" on the map. Beyond its borders dwell all those I must never again attempt to contact, because I am toxic to their wellbeing. There are more of these than you might imagine. I have always found it easier to permanently end relationships than deal with the realities of their changing. The first appearance of such a Perilous Realm, in my literary life at least, is a poem of mine dating from 1984:

> And through my lands you softly came;
> exploring scenes
> you'd once conceived as if amazed at what a
> little time
> had wrought: found shadows cast about my
> heart by
> trees formidable. I wished you would by some
> judicial felling let the summer in, but I lay
> impotent as mountains and could only watch
> you turn
> dismayed, a little disillusioned,
> to some fresher view.

> From: "What Happened to the Lovetrees?"

In different guise, the realm appears in a short story of mine titled *Poser V1.0*. The Tolkien references are deliberate.

> One part of her realm she had not revisited, though she could not fully purge it from her mind. It was a region like none other in her demesne: a region mazed in enchantments. Protected from invasion and escape by a forest of thorns, their savage spears sheathed in clouds of crimson flowers. Within the bounds of that little realm a man languished endlessly, lost in the bitterness of unsatiated lust.

This is not healthy placement of boundaries, it is wall building born out of fear. A recent conversation with Fran touched on this. We were talking about how she manages to release her hold on difficult, even toxic, relationships without forever banishing the other person to the Forbidden Zone. I have seen this in practice several times over the course of our friendship.

> Fran: This is why I don't give up on people.
>
> Martin: I have learned to let go.
>
> Fran: Giving up is different than letting go.
>
> Martin: I was just pondering that. I'm not sure. Maybe.
>
> Fran: Giving up implies hopeless. Letting go implies openness. Open handedness.

Martin: Closing the door, vs leaving it open?

Fran: Yes.

Martin: It's not always healthy to leave the door open. (That's what I'm thinking, anyway, about me and my relationships.)

Fran: It's ok to close the door but not the heart.

I still have work to do in this area. It is the primary relationship challenge for me for the year ahead. There are many other aspects of being "Well-boundaried," including its relevance to co-dependency and self-care. I may return to the topic another time. If you are interested in the subject, I recommend the work of Brené Brown.

[MB]

When I Am Happy I Make Soup

Published January 14, 2017

When I am happy I make soup
When I am down I make soup
When there's drama I make soup
When there's peace I make soup
Then, I have to give.

[FH]

It's Not Just for Kids: Reading Together for Fun and Friendship

Published January 25, 2017

"The most important sounds we can ever share with another person are our own voices."

THE ABOVE QUOTATION is from the chapter in our book where we discuss how we make our 3,000 mile, transatlantic, friendship work. We believe there are many kinds of distance that can separate people, and not all are measured in miles or time zones. What keeps our relationship fresh and alive is our willingness to keep the channels of communication open between us, no matter what.

Reading together is one way we honor that commitment, and among the most rewarding. Young children, and their parents, know this instinctively. And yet as adults we rarely read to one another. When was the last time you read to your adult child, to your partner, or to a friend? Geography need not be an obstacle. Fran and I live on opposite sides of the world, yet read together regularly on our video calls. We do this both for simple pleasure, and because Fran finds it helpful. She has difficulty maintaining focus and finds lengthy works easier to digest if they are read to her.

Borrowing the phrase which introduced each story on *Listen with Mother* (a BBC children's radio program which ran between 1950 and 1982), I begin each reading with the words: "Are you sitting [or lying] comfortably? Then I'll begin." This simple formula marks the occasion as something special, and helps us focus on the words we are about to share.

Since we met online in 2011, we have enjoyed a wide range of fiction and non-fiction books, including thrillers by suspense novelist James Hayman. As Fran says: "There is nothing better than a well-written thriller.. and nothing better than it being set in your hometown.. and actually knowing the author.. but when you have an Englishman reading it to you.. that takes the cake.."

In addition to James Hayman's thrillers *The Girl in the Glass, Darkness First, The Chill of Night,* and *The Cutting,* we've read *The Stone Trilogy (The Distant Shore, Under the Same Sun, Song of the Storm)* by Mariam Kobras, and Donna Tartt's *The Goldfinch.* Nonfiction titles include:

- *Daring Greatly* and *Rising Strong,* by Brené Brown
- *Savor: Mindful Eating, Mindful Life,* by Thich Nhat Hanh and Dr. Lilian Cheung
- *An Unquiet Mind,* by Kay Redfield Jamison
- *Say Goodnight to Insomnia,* by Gregg D. Jacobs

A full length novel or nonfiction book can take weeks to read, and represents a significant commitment in time and energy. Shorter works, collections, and poetry (including my own *Collected Poems*) can be dipped into at any time. Those we've enjoyed include some perennial favourites:

- *The Little Prince,* by Antoine de Saint-Exupéry
- *The Velveteen Rabbit,* by Margery Williams
- *The Happy Prince and Other Tales,* by Oscar Wilde
- *The Prophet,* by Khalil Gibran
- *Winnie-the-Pooh,* by A. A. Milne

We keep a list of web pages, newspaper articles, and blog posts to read when we get chance. For the past three years we've subscribed to the Compassion Course Online offered by the New York Center for Nonviolent Communication. Each week we read the latest lesson together and discuss its relevance to our lives.

Although I do most of the reading, it's not all one way. Fran reads me pieces she finds; she also reads back to me the letters I write her. We read aloud to each other a good deal throughout the process of writing our book, especially the editing and proofreading phases.

Reading together has given us confidence to read in public. I've read excerpts from *High Tide, Low Tide* at the Newcastle Literary Salon, and we've read at public events including a panel discussion on mental health and social media, and a fundraiser for non-profit Family Hope.

Whether they are your words or another's, whether the person you're sharing them with is in the same room as you or on the other side of the world, reading to someone can be a powerful, beautiful, and empowering act. It is also an antidote to personal separation. As we say in our book *High Tide, Low Tide*:

> No matter the nature of distance in your friendship, keep in touch. Keep talking. Keep the channels open and the communication flowing. Share your time, your thoughts, and your worlds. Do that, and closeness will never be far away.

[MB]

Lifting the Curtain: Brightness, Joy, and Vigilance

Published April 11, 2017

AS I WRITE THIS, Fran is heading out to a gallery opening in Portland, and then to a classical guitar concert. Before she left, she said to me: "I feel so good.. it's really strange.. my mind is thinking thoughts that are good.. and it's effortless.."

After months, first of depression and then debilitating fatigue, it's still early days, but something does seem to have shifted — or rather, to be shifting.

It is wonderful to see the light in her eyes again. To sense hope again. To witness the transition from darkness into light once more.

We are both aware of the need for vigilance. Bipolar is like that. Any brightness, any momentary joy, each lifting of the curtain, is suspect, and may be the prelude to mania. But as I told Fran today: "You are doing well, and it feels wholesome to me. We will be vigilant. But don't be scared to have a nice time, to smile, to find ease and enjoyment. These things are your right. You are worthy of them; of goodness, of living life fully."

[MB]

Like a Rootless Tree (Where Are Your Roots?)

Published June 7, 2017

"SO, WHERE *ARE* YOUR ROOTS?"

It's not every day you get asked a question like that in the gents' toilet at Bar Loco. At least, it's not every day *I* get asked that in the gents' toilet at Bar Loco. Then again, I'm not there very often. It was the t-shirt, of course. My American Roots t-shirt. Specifically, given I was standing at the urinal, the back of the shirt which asks WHERE ARE YOUR ROOTS? in sans serif caps. Caught off-guard, mid-pee, I stumbled for an answer.

"Well," I said, looking down at my chest. "I'm not American. The shirt is. It was a gift from my bestie in Maine. I'm from Liverpool."

"Cheshire," my new friend responded.

"Erm." Zipping up and turning to see who I was addressing. "Merseyside."

"Cheshire." He asserted, smiling.

I knew he was wrong. Liverpool was in Lancashire when I was growing up, until 1974 when I became a teenager and Liverpool became a part of the metropolitan county of Merseyside. But I didn't feel confident enough to contradict him without googling it to check, and somehow I didn't feel right doing that just then.

Our impromptu conversation (I was washing my hands by this stage) moved on to my Scouse accent — or rather, my lack of one. My sister is fiercely proud of her accent. My mother hates to be reminded of hers. I am indifferent. My accent was never strong, and I've not spent any significant time in Liverpool since I left at 18.

I was at University in Bradford for four years. London for three. Six months in Norwich staying in the nurses' home at the Norfolk & Norwich Hospital (which sounds racier than it was, me not being a very racy chap). Thirty years and counting here in Newcastle. I've picked up a little dialect and inflection here and there. Talking on Skype with Fran three hours a day for six years has added an American twist or two. I frequently find myself somewhere mid-Atlantic, poised between tomahto and tomayto, shedule and skedule. Especially when reading aloud to Fran, which I do a lot. Especially reading books by American authors (ditto, we know a few). But that's another story.

Where was I?

Ah yes. Bar Loco. I was there for the Newcastle Literary Salon spoken word event, and this month's theme was "PLACE AND IDENTITY."

You can see where this is going — which is more than I've ever been able to do, really. I've never had much idea where I was heading. Not so much drifting as carried by whatever currents were in play at the time. Only in the past few years have I gained any sense of direction. Of purpose. Of — now I come to think about it — rootedness.

> *Rootedness*: Noun. The quality or state of having roots, especially of being firmly established, settled, or entrenched.

Aside: this post's title comes from the Damien Rice song "Like a Rootless Tree," specifically the version with Lisa Hannigan. If you don't know it, listen to it now. You will thank me. Really. As a friend of mine said, "I fucking LOVE this song!" (The expletive is deliberate, you'll understand when you listen to it.) Several of those performing at the Salon, poets for the most part, had borrowed from song lyrics or titles in the pieces they shared. So I'm in good company.

I've attended most of the Salon events over the past year. I've performed three times, reading excerpts from our book, *High Tide, Low Tide*. This time, though, I was there to listen. To open myself to the frequently raw, gutsy passion of those who dare to bare and share at the mic. I've written before how potent and challenging the Salon is for me.

I wasn't disappointed. One after the other, I was moved by performer and performance alike. Aidan Clarke, whose voice I would willingly drown in. Melissa Chaplin, who spoke of her own issues with dialect and accent. Iain Rowan's performance resonated especially. He spoke of how our roots need not be limited to the places we grew up in; they can be all the places and connections we have made in our journey through life. And that got me thinking. Or rather, it got me feeling. Always a good thing for a writer to hear, so I hope Iain gets to read this.

I've never felt much attachment to my city and region of birth. My one remaining attachment to Liverpool is my mother. Despite having other family there, I know that when my mother dies I will never revisit. There will be nothing there for me. Nothing there of me. For me, places are rendered meaningful not by accident of birth or count of years, but by virtue of the events and relationships they held or hold.

Iain's poem, *We Planets, We Comets*, recounted a summer of earnest and joyful friendship. It recalled university days and months — and poetry — of my own.

In the REAL WORLD nothing rhymes and no
one cares
yet here
still, even
the furniture loves us.
Maybe we're right
but know we'll never leave this place
our place though fortunes raze our hopes
erase our friends and set our eager souls
dutifully.

From "for Richard's room."

That's part of my rootedness, for sure. Bradford. One house in particular. Where else? One cottage in Wales. A London bedsit. Our holiday cottage at Brough. Evening walks to Great Musgrave along "Memory Lane." Keep 'em coming. The waiting room at the QEII Cruise Terminal in Southampton. Brayloo.

I'm liking this sense of rootedness Iain has gifted me! Roots don't have to be where we were born or grew up. They are — or can be — collected along the way and carried around with us.

In which case, my rootedness (I see this now), includes places I've never travelled. Not in person. Not in the flesh. But virtually (whatever that means) as Fran's armchair travel buddy, tagging along in her pocket by the magic of Skype and instant messaging. Spain. Germany. Austria. Amsterdam. Peaks Island. Portland, Maine: a city I feel at home in despite my feet never having touched the sidewalk. Never having touched the pavement.

It's a fundamental tenet of my relationship with Fran and the work we're doing in the mental health arena that physical distance need not preclude deep, meaningful and successful relationships. Our vision is a world where no one is too far away to be cared for or to care.

I once asked Fran what I contributed most to our friendship. She gave me the image of an oak tree, standing strong and tall. At the time, I hadn't felt too grounded, solid, rooted. Looking back now, I can see things differently.

Rather than imagining myself rootless, I can choose to see myself, to feel myself, part of a network with roots deep and wide enough to encompass the globe. (Think oaks, not baobabs: a nod to the wisdom of Antoine de Saint-Exupéry's *Little Prince*, who attended to the toilet of his tiny planet as we would be well advised to attend to the toilet of ours.)

Speaking of toilets, next time I'm in the gents at Bar Loco I'm going to be prepared. I know where my roots are.

[MB]

BESIEGED: Sometimes I Just Want to Be Left Alone

Published July 12, 2017

IT'S SATURDAY MORNING and as I often am, I'm sitting in my favorite coffee shop, Caffè Nero near the Haymarket in Newcastle. I've been coming here regularly since it opened. How many years is that? Before Fran and I began work on our book, for sure, and that's pushing five years now.

It's hard to visualize, but this used to be the City Post Office. I've stood in line many times — where these tables are now — for postage stamps, or to send packages off all over the world. It looks so different now! And yet, there is a sense of continuity. I may have to go elsewhere these days for my postal services (as I did this morning, to buy stamps and to mail out a copy of our book) but it is here, a large black coffee to hand ("Would you like the extra shot?" "Yes please!"), that I write my letters, cards, and postcards.

Here is also where I meet folk face-to-face. Caffè Nero is my social hub these days. The staff have changed over the years, but have always been warm, personable, and supportive of my mental health work and our book. If I am meeting someone in town, here is my first choice of venue, and I have made several new friends from amongst the other regulars here. Last Saturday, a friend I know from elsewhere turned up unexpectedly. We had a great conversation, and hope to meet up again soon.

For years, I had no one local to meet up with for a drink and a chat. I recall sitting in a different coffee bar, not far from here, aware that no one I knew was likely to walk in, whether accidentally or by arrangement, to greet me with a smile or a hug and share time with me over a cup of coffee.

Nowadays, I bump into people all the time! Folk I have met here at Caffè Nero, or from the monthly Literary Salon at Bar Loco (which I only learned about last year from a guy I got chatting to at Nero's) or through Time to Change and Broadacre House. I have opened myself up to the world, and the world has opened to greet me.

But, sometimes, it all gets a bit much. Sometimes I just want to sit here and not be talked to, especially when I am clearly writing. Sometimes it's nice to be anonymous. To be ignored. Sometimes it's nice to be gifted a "Hi, nice to see you" without my "Hi" back being taken as an invitation to occupy my space for the next twenty minutes.

So, this morning when it happened I kept my head down. Finished the letter I was writing, and kept right on going, lest any pause in my writing signal a willingness to engage. I drafted a new blog piece. This one.

And now that I am no longer besieged I can relax again. Breathe. I guess I need to work on my boundaries, but at least something good came of the experience.

[MB]

Welcome Home! Post-Vacation Support for the Bipolar Traveler

Published November 22, 2017

THE TRAVELER with bipolar disorder faces a number of challenges. Leaving behind proven routines and support structures, the journeying itself (especially if different time zones are involved), and the excitement of new places and opportunities are all intrinsically destabilizing. Good planning, including a Travel Wellness Plan, goes a long way to mitigate the risks. Factoring in some post-vacation support is valuable too.

In our book, *High Tide, Low Tide*, Fran and I describe how we managed our mutually supportive friendship whilst Fran was touring Europe with her elderly parents, as well as what happened on her return home. On that occasion, Fran couldn't rest and recuperate, as she had to immediately look for somewhere new to live, pack up, and move home. Fortunately, not every trip is quite so traumatic!

Fran has just returned from a ten day vacation with a friend to Edisto Beach in South Carolina: a round trip of 2,200 miles. She arrived home last night around 6 p.m. her time (11 p.m. for me here in the UK). We met on webcam shortly afterwards. Fran had warned me in advance not to expect too much from her on this first call. The journey north had taken two days, and the 22-hour drive had been compounded by car troubles and a less than satisfactory motel stopover. (Note to self: pay more attention to online reviews when suggesting travel accommodation!)

I imagined we'd be on for no more than ten or fifteen minutes: long enough for me to welcome her back and to briefly catch up on anything immediately pressing. Anything else could and would have to wait. As it turned out, our call lasted an hour and a half. Fran was exhausted, but needed me to hold space for her to release what she was feeling and thinking, so she could unwind. I got to contribute, but we agreed I would have my turn later. This first call was for her. We had our usual check in at midday my time today and will meet later on webcam. There is no specific agenda, but as we move through these first post-vacation days we will be focused on a few key areas.

Vigilance

It's more difficult to help Fran keep an eye on her health when she's away from home. We kept in regular touch on this trip using chat, and had a few voice and video calls, but far fewer and shorter than usual. Getting back to our usual structure is stabilizing in itself and will help each of us assess how Fran's doing in terms of her physical, mental, and emotional wellbeing.

Catch up

I have a fair idea what Fran did while she was away, because she shared things with me day-to-day and on her social media. But, as I mentioned to her last night, "I've had ten days of life, too!" I look forward to sharing my news with Fran and hearing more of what she took away from her vacation.

Processing

We approach any experience as an opportunity for growth and learning. This curiosity has stood us in good stead in the past. We will take time over the coming days and weeks to explore what we've experienced while Fran has been away, celebrate our successes, and look for lessons learned. For example, Fran mastered a new GPS app, and successfully navigated the route to and from Edisto, as well as on day trips through the week. She and her friend also handled spending most of their time together on the trip, including four days on the road. Being in less frequent contact always offers opportunities to explore connection, independence, and co-dependency in our relationship, and this trip was no exception.

Picking up the reins

We parked a number of things while Fran was away, so we will review these and pick up where we need to. This includes appointments, preparing for upcoming events and trips, and the holiday season (Thanksgiving, Christmas, and New Year).

Hanging out

One of the things I am most looking forward to is hanging out again with Fran, especially reading together. We are currently reading *Outlander* by Diana Gabaldon and working through all eleven series of the American sitcom *Cheers* on TV. Fran loves to travel, when funds and circumstances allow. We are already planning for further trips next year. With care and forethought, we know she can travel safely. And with some dedicated post-vacation support, we know we can grow and move forward, both stronger for the experience. [MB]

What If We Treated Problems with Our Bodies and Minds Like We Treat Our Tech?

Published December 27, 2017

FRAN AND I live on opposite sides of the Atlantic. We use technology. A lot. Without it, we couldn't do our friendship at all. Indeed, we would never have met. Fran has a Windows laptop and an iPhone. I have a Samsung Android phone, a PC, and a Chromebook. I like Google drive for sharing documents and cloud storage. Fran prefers OneDrive and her iCloud. Connecting might be simpler if we agreed to use the same technologies and platforms, but we get by and learn a lot in the process.

One way or another, technology is an integral part of our everyday lives, whether at work or at home or out and about in the world. Computers. Phones. Cameras. TV. Wi-Fi. Internet banking. Shopping. Entertainment.

We have some basic (and probably incorrect) ideas about how it all hangs together. We want it to work most of the time and grumble when it doesn't, but we accept there are going to be difficulties and do our best to work around them.

When problems and complications arise, we don't think worse of ourselves or each other for having them. We talk to each other. We reach out for assistance, confident someone we know will have had similar experiences or know someone who might be able to help. We've all had our home Wi-Fi crash on us for no apparent reason, our phones die at crucial moments, or our home printers refuse to cooperate with us. We empathize and offer support to one another. We share fixes and workarounds. We understand because tech is really, really, complicated. It would be silly to expect it to work perfectly all the time.

Wouldn't it be great if we had the same attitude toward our bodies, emotions, and brains? Because if our phones, computers, and TVs are complex, we are gloriously more so.

[MB]

Our Mexican Adventure, Part One: "I Got My Crew"

Posted January 24, 2018

"I give myself permission to fully experience whatever comes up during this trip, knowing I am safe."

IN OUR BOOK, *High Tide, Low Tide: The Caring Friend's Guide to Bipolar Disorder*, Fran and I describe how we handled our distance, mutually supportive, friendship while she was traveling in Europe for three months in 2013. Fran has taken a few shorter trips since then, but nothing comparable in terms of length, distance, or potential impact on her health and wellbeing. Until now.

Right now, she is newly arrived in Mexico for a month to undertake dental work. I thought it would be interesting to blog my side of things in a series of weekly posts. In this first post, we move through the week leading up to Fran's arrival in Guadalajara.

Tuesday, 16 January 2018, 7:40 a.m. UK time
Fran and I were both tired when we met on Skype last night (Monday). I was tired from my day at work and then my evening meeting with Time to Change and Cygnus to discuss possible mental health initiatives in Northumberland. Fran was tired from a day that had been filled with people. She'd enjoyed the connections (lunch with a friend, and various online and phone conversations), but she realised another day had slipped by without having made a start on her packing. That definitely needs to start today!

Tuesday. Wednesday. Thursday. Friday. Saturday. Five days left to get everything done. Which we will! The great thing is, Fran is aware she needs to allow space/time for resting as well as doing. So, after we'd talked about our respective days, I read to her (*Outlander*) and we watched some *Midsomer Murders* on Netflix until it was time to say good night, a little earlier than usual.

I wasn't feeling too good myself yesterday, and sort of dumped that on Fran in the afternoon when I was deciding if I was up to going to the mental health event. Today, I will hold myself open to whatever Fran needs me to help her with, which will probably include packing this evening. We got this.

Wednesday, 17 January 2018, 7:40 a.m. UK time
Well, Fran didn't get any work done on her packing or finances yesterday (Tuesday), so those have moved into today. (It is a "snow day" in Portland today and she doesn't intend to go out at all.) Yesterday she went to her Forever Fit class, and to her massage appointment. We did do some important emails for the trip, including arranging transport from Guadalajara to Ajijic next week. I did try to encourage/insist that we do at least a little packing when we met at 11 p.m. (her 6 p.m.), but Fran was adamant she didn't want to, so we had a talk instead, and some reading, and watched a David Attenborough wildlife show on Netflix.

We also had another attempt at getting the MiFi device to work, but it's not connecting. I found some more detailed notes online which we can try at some point. Frustrating, that it doesn't work, but we are not anticipating needing to use it. I think I will see if there is another 21-day meditation challenge in the next few weeks. That is something I could do, as part of my self-care plan.

Thursday, 18 January 2018, 7:35 a.m. UK time
I don't think Fran's done any actual putting-things-in-the-suitcase packing yet, BUT she had a very productive day yesterday (Wednesday): finances, emails etc. and I have no doubt she is on track for Sunday. We've had to accept defeat on the MiFi front. We followed the additional instructions last night but still no "green light." We went through the To Do list together. It is mostly all done now. And overnight Fran heard back from Dental Express to confirm they can drive her from Guadalajara to Ajijic on Tuesday.

I'm also pleased with how I am preparing for the next four weeks. I have this journal/log which will feed my blogging, and my list of Things I Would Quite Like to Do to keep me on track. I know I will really feel it when Fran and I are less in touch than usual, especially at the times we are usually on Skype. I give myself permission to feel whatever comes up, and not hold on too tight to it.

FEEL IT.
CLAIM IT.
LOVE IT.
LET IT GO.

Friday, 19 January 2018, 7:35 a.m. UK time
Fran is well on track now! She carried her laptop on a little tour of the apartment last night while we were on Skype so I could see how she is getting all her clothes, meds, and other things ready for the trip. She is stepping

steadily though these final days, doing what she needs to, and resting, too.

We read together (*Outlander*) and watched more of *Planet Earth*. Fran is blown away by the programme in all its aspects: the teams who go out to capture the footage, the production teams, Attenborough himself … It feeds her sense of wonder and is a great reminder (re-minder) to me, to stay in the moment. To pay attention to what is going on.

I'm feeling prepared for the next few weeks. I found a talk by a mental health author called Lucy Nichol at Waterstones bookstore in March and booked a ticket. Good to have some things ahead in my calendar. Stepping stones through the year, and maybe some friends will want to go too.

Saturday, 20 January 2018, 10 a.m. UK time
Yesterday, I compiled my personal Wellness Plan for the Mexico trip, and printed it out so I can keep it to hand in my journal. I am excited about seeing how we (I) do. Fran got lots more done through the morning, and had everything to hand to do the physical packing when we had our Skype at 7 p.m. (her 2 p.m.) She had been concerned not everything would fit into her luggage, but it did! As she packed things, I marked them off on our packing list, and afterwards read it back to her so we knew we'd not missed anything.

We did her suitcase and backpack in about 40 minutes, and did the rest when we met again later. Fran was so delighted and relieved that everything fit! It was a big weight off her shoulders. We did have a couple of scares. There was an earthquake in the Mexico region, although not especially close to where we are going. And a friend shared a travel advisory notice which was a bit scary, but fortunately it seems to be okay in Jalisco. We will remain vigilant, but we are going!

Sunday, 21 January 2018, 1 p.m. UK time

Last night Fran and I met for our final pre-Mexico Skype call. There was nothing really to do, but we read through our packing and To Do lists one last time just to be sure. We talked a little about how the journey might go, acutely aware of the significance of this trip to us both. I told her I am ready for it from my point of view. I have my Wellness Plan, and I am curious too, which is always a healthy way to approach change. We watched another episode of *Planet Earth*, then said good night.

This morning I messaged her as we'd arranged, to make sure she was up for our friend Beth to drive her to the bus station. She was already awake. I double checked she was actually up out of bed, and that she'd packed the very final things, including her phone charger and cables. She had. She messaged me just before leaving her apartment.

"I am as ready as I can be. A bit scared too. Today's Angel Card is 'Awakening'."

Later, talking about the trip as a whole, she said: "I will feel fear. I will counter it with being present."

Beth was on time and stayed with Fran until she was on the bus (thank you, Beth!) During the drive to Boston, Fran got a bit unsure about gate numbers for her flights, so I looked them up on the United Airlines app.

"I can't imagine doing any of this without you."

"You're stuck with me now, Frannie. Didn't you know that?"

Monday, 22 January 2018, 07:35 a.m. UK time

Fran messaged me just now, as I headed out of the house on my way to work. She is safe in her hotel room in Guadalajara ("Hotel Frances is gorgeous"), but it was a hell of a journey for her yesterday. The first leg, Boston–Newark, went fine, but the next departure was delayed which meant she couldn't catch her final scheduled flight to Guadalajara. The replacement flight was also delayed, so that she didn't land in Mexico until around 20 past midnight local time.

I stayed with Fran most of the way. We couldn't chat when she was in the air of course, but I tracked the flights (and the delays!) via the United Airlines app and website. I messaged the hotel to let them know Fran would be late. I'm not sure if they got the message (Fran also tried to call them with no success), but it all worked out in the end. Fran was also concerned about how she would get to the hotel so late at night. It was about a 30 minute drive from the airport. This was something I couldn't help with, so she posted in one of the Ajijic Facebook groups for suggestions:

> My flight into Guadalajara tonight got delayed by three hours, so I land at midnight. I had planned on using Uber but am wondering if anyone has a trusted driver willing to drive me from the airport to Hotel Frances. I am ecstatic about spending a month in Ajijic and meeting some of you!

People in the group were really helpful and supportive: a great example of using a wider support network when needed. I kept Fran company on chat while she waited at Houston for her final flight, which was also delayed.

"I just checked online, Fran. They're waiting for crew."

"I got my crew — you."

It was around 3:20 a.m. my time when she boarded and we said good night. ("Thanks for staying with me." "Of course.")

So … she is in her room in "her" hotel (Hotel Frances) in Guadalajara. Exhausted, but safe. She's taken her meds (we've agreed that I will remind her to take them for at least the next few days as she settles into her new routine). She doesn't have her luggage, and the AT&T data package for her phone doesn't seem to be working yet, but hopefully both those issues will be resolved later today.

We are here (HERENOW). That's what matters.

Tuesday, 23 January 2018, 7:30 a.m. UK time

I had a few chat conversations with Fran through the day yesterday (Monday), and a lovely Skype call in the evening. It was just 10 minutes or so but it grounded me and gave me a handle on how she's doing. She was really tired, of course, but she'd had a good time being shown around Guadalajara by a friend of hers who lives there. She took lots of great photos, too.

Fran was reunited with her luggage: it was delivered to her hotel in the afternoon. Her data/phone are also working now. I had a great chat session with Daniel on the AT&T support line. As well as providing the technical help we needed (it was a setting on Fran's phone we'd forgotten about), Daniel was really nice and friendly. He commented that Fran and I were clearly good friends, which led to a conversation about our book and the website and the journal/blog I am doing for the trip. I said he might even get a mention, so here you go, Daniel!

When Fran and I had our call it was around 5 p.m. Mexico time. Fran was about to have a rest and was considering going for a stroll later. In the end, she decided to focus on self-care. I know she wanted to make the most of being in Guadalajara, but she recognised her body needed to rest.

"I thought about going out, but there would be lots of people, and the sun is setting. I thought about going downstairs to the bar or restaurant but there's lots of people. I've had people all day Sunday and today. So I think staying in and resting feels like what I need to do. Tomorrow morning I'll explore, but tonight is mine. I don't need to push myself."

Today (Tuesday) a car provided by Dental Express will collect Fran from her hotel and drive her to Ajijic, which is about an hour south of Guadalajara, on the north shore of Lake Chapala. She will collect the keys to her friend's apartment and can then finally unpack and relax. It's been quite a week. I'm so proud of her.

Hey, Fran — you did it (we did it)! We're in Mexico!

[MB]

Our Mexican Adventure, Part Two: "Well, the Good Thing Is ..."

Posted January 31, 2018

THIS POST COVERS Fran's first week in the town of Ajijic in the State of Jalisco, on the north shore of Lake Chapala, Mexico.

Wednesday, 24 January 2018, 7:35 a.m. UK time

I had a nice call with Fran yesterday (Tuesday). She'd slept better (the first night she'd woken freezing cold and had to put on extra layers), and sounded calm. She was glad she'd decided to stay in and rest the night before. The call set us both up for the day. Fran went out for brunch in Guadalajara yesterday, checked out from Hotel Frances at noon and then caught her ride to Ajijic ("Hola, Enrique!") She picked up the keys to the apartment, and started to get settled in.

Unfortunately, when she unpacked she discovered one of her tops has gone missing from her suitcase. She was understandably upset and it did nothing to help her feel at ease.

"I'm nervous about this whole trip. My Bali top going missing really pissed me off, along with all the other things. I brought my best ones, goddammit. I should have brought the old ones. I cannot get these any more. They don't make them."

"… all the other things" include some issues with her phone charger. I'm not sure what is up with that, but she will be able to charge her phone and her back-up battery pack via the PC at the apartment if necessary. She enjoyed dinner at her friend's place, though. She let me know when she got home.

"Back.. horizontal.. whew.. Evening was fun.. Ted walked me home.."

Her choice of words didn't escape my notice.

"That's nice, Fran. It is home, for the next few weeks."

Wednesday, 24 January 2018, 1:30 p.m. UK time

"I've had enough now."

"Shall I send the helicopter?"

"Yes, please."

That's how our phone call began just now. Despite how it sounds, Fran's hanging in there. It's just all very new and also very exhausting for her. She plans to meet up with friends again today at some point, possibly for a jaunt to Chapala market, and then dinner this evening. The issue with the phone charger doesn't seem too bad after all. It might just be a dodgy connection. Fran took two plugs and several USB cables, so she should be okay.

Thursday, 25 January 2018, 7:30 a.m. UK time

Fran went out exploring yesterday (Wednesday) afternoon. She got a bit lost when she went looking for a particular coffee bar / café, but a nice lady helped her out and she got there in the end. It threw her a bit, though. Later on, back at her apartment, we had a great video call, our first of this trip. She gave me a tour of the apartment and I also got to see the mountains! Seeing it all live helps me get a feel for where (and how) she is.

And how is she? I'm not going to say she's struggling, but she isn't settled in yet and things like getting a bit lost, and not knowing the language, and her

Bali top going missing, and having a bit of a sore tummy, all add up to her not enjoying it as much as she'd like to. She's also uncertain about how it will be once her friends return from their vacation tomorrow (Friday), so she no longer has the apartment all to herself. On the other hand, that could help her. She is feeling a bit … not lonely, but on her own having to do things, make plans and decisions herself. She's travelled on her own before, but not for quite a while, and the times I'm thinking of (trips to Europe before I met her) were distinctly mania-fuelled. Thankfully, that is not the case this time. She said last night she's realised she prefers traveling with a companion. (Yes, I am with her, but it's not the same.)

As for me, I'm doing okay! Last evening I read some more of the book *Talk Like TED*, and chatted online with a few folk. I had a beer, watched some TV, and had an early night. I am keeping busy, but also allowing space and time for myself. My Wellness Plan helps. I have referred to it a few times and it helps keep me on track.

At work today (Thursday) I learned about a Mental Health First Aid (MHFA) course they are putting on in March. I put my name down for it (at my boss' insistence, she is incredibly supportive of all my mental health work). It's four years since I took the course and I'd love to refresh my skills. I am encouraging colleagues to consider it too.

Friday, 26 January 2018, 7:35 a.m. UK time
Fran and I Skyped twice yesterday (Thursday) evening. On the first call, I helped compile and send the first of her "postcard" emails to friends. I downloaded the photos we'd selected from her iCloud, and resized them in Photoshop. We emailed them out, and also posted them to

Facebook. Fran only has her phone to work on and it's easier for me to do the fiddly bits on my PC.

Time to fess up! I got rather frustrated and grumpy when the technology wouldn't work the way we wanted it to. Fran stayed calm, though, rather than getting cross at me for getting cross. That helped me move through what I was feeling without it blowing up into more than it was. Fran is tired, for sure, and feeling a bit "off," but she wrote something today which shows how well she is handling things.

"It hasn't all been easy but my new mantra is 'Well, the good thing is …' That way I can turn it around and be ok with whatever is. Ajijic is a simple sweet town with lots of color and complexity. I'm glad to be experiencing all that it is."

When we met later we checked through Fran's spending, and then put "work" aside and just hung out for a while. This included me reading some more of *Outlander*. I imagine it's the first time this story of 18th Century Scotland, written by an American, has been read in the UK by a Brit to an American in Mexico!

Saturday, 27 January 2018, 11:00 a.m. UK time
Fran and I had a nice voice call last night (Friday) at around 11 p.m. (her 5 p.m.). She'd been out and about throughout the day, including visiting one lovely looking café (Casa del Cafe) after another place she'd gone to had been closed. I was looking through some of her photos and bounced one back to her that I especially liked.

"Oh, this is gorgeous, Fran."

"That's where I am right now!"

Later, she met up with her two hosts, who had returned from vacation. After spending some time with them, Fran retired to her room, which is where we had our call. We talked about what we'd been up to and our plans for the next few days. In Fran's case that included a boat trip today (Saturday) to Scorpion Island, and a visit to some hot springs on Monday with a lady she's met here. We need to research the hot springs a bit before then!

I feel we are doing really well: individually, and as a team. I spent my time last evening working on the website, and I started reading the *30-Day Book Marketing Challenge*, by Rachel Thompson, which arrived yesterday. I was immediately inspired to update the cover image and bio on my Twitter account, so I figure it's already working!

When I came into town today (Saturday), I planned to go to the Starbucks across the road from Central Station, only it was full. I went back into the station to check the other coffee bars, but they were also pretty busy. So, I stomped off to walk to the library. I could feel myself getting stressed and angry because things weren't going the way I'd wanted them to. But I remembered my Wellness Plan, and Fran's "dropping the hot coal" strategy. It worked! I could feel the stress leave me as I walked. I thought also of how Fran had handled having to change her plans for a burger the day before, when the first place she chose was shut. She is generally better than me at this stuff, but I'm rather proud, how I handled things this morning!

Saturday, 27 January 2018, 2:45 p.m. UK time

I'm at Costa Coffee in Blackwell's Bookshop, and just had a fun video call with Fran! It was 8:45 a.m. for Fran, and the house cleaner was due at 9 a.m. so we didn't have very long, but it was good to catch up. She went out to a local festival last night with one of her friends, then for something to eat which included some kind of "Aztec soup" and a "medium" beer that turned out to be huge!

Sunday, 28 January 2018, 1:10 p.m. UK time

There's not much to write today as we didn't get to have any more calls yesterday (Saturday) with Fran out all day on her trip to the island. I've seen her photos and I'd say she had a good time. We did chat a bit, though. Fran messaged me this yesterday evening.

"I don't have anything planned for Sunday except TSA [completing her compensation claim for the loss of her Bali top] and photo processing. You will be blown away. It will be hard to choose."

"That's cool. I can help with that if you want."

"Yep. Are you keeping track of my activities day by day?"

"Yes. That's what's in my journal, and will be in the weekly blogs."

"I'm settling into this new place and people."

That final comment is so important, and so healthy. One week ago, Fran was on her outward journey from Portland to Guadalajara. It's been quite a week for us both! But she's doing fine. I am too. Last night (Saturday) I typed up my Mexico journal notes and started working them into what will be this week's blog post. I watched some TV, chatted with friends online, and watched a documentary on YouTube.

Monday, 29 January 2018, 12:00 p.m. UK time

Fran and I met twice yesterday (Sunday). On our first call I shared what had been happening in my world. We then looked over her to do list for the day, which included getting her latest photos sent out to her "postcard" mailing list and posted to Facebook. Between us we selected ten photos: quite a challenge as there were loads of great ones! I downloaded them to my PC and resized them in Photoshop. We also composed a reply to an email from TSA (Transportation Security Administration) regarding Fran's compensation claim for the top that went missing from her luggage. When we met up again later, Fran was in a local blues bar!

"Shall we do the TSA and photo things now? I plan to show you Ajijic after."

It took a little while but the emails and posting to Facebook went smoothly, and without me getting all frustrated like I had earlier in the week!

With our chores done, Fran took me on a Skype walkabout through the streets of the town. It was wonderful to see all the sights; the colourful buildings, the people, the murals, the dog and horse poop. We ended up at the market in the plaza, which was buzzing with people. No one seemed remotely phased at the sight of Fran holding her phone up to the side of her head as we walked and talked together. Well, apart from one little girl in the market who did look at us a bit funny!

Then Fran bumped into someone she knew who invited her to join his party for dinner. Fran at first said thanks, maybe another time, but then changed her mind and dropped me to take up the invitation. Maybe I was being petty, but it really hurt. I could have kept it to myself, but that's not how we do things, so after calming down a bit I messaged Fran to share how I was feeling.

"Oh shit.. I'm so sorry.. It was just in the moment.. I didn't mean to make you feel that way."

"It hurt, to be dropped like that."

"I realize that. I would've felt the same way. I was trying to make it special then I fucked up."

"It was special, Fran. I fuck up sometimes, too! It's ok. I just needed you to know."

"It was fun carrying you around. We'll do it again."

It was pretty late by then, and we said good night. I thought about it a lot on my way into work this morning. I got to be honest. Fran got to be honest. We both got a bit hurt, but there was no lasting harm. It's what we do. I realised too that there was more going on for me last night than just having our conversation cut short. I've been feeling pressured lately in various ways. I'd looked forward to chilling out with Fran and things didn't work out the way I'd hoped. (In NVC terms, my needs weren't met.) That's the top and bottom of it, really. I've not been taking very good care of my boundaries.

With this in mind, I decided to give myself some space today and posted this up on my Facebook: as much as a reminder to myself as anything/anyone else.

A bit overwhelmed with stuff at the moment.
If you are waiting to hear from me I will get
back to you when I can. Feel free to nudge me
but I may not respond straight away. Thanks.

I will spend some time with my Wellness Plan today. It will serve us both well.

Tuesday, 30 January 2018, 07:30 a.m. UK time
What a difference a day can make! I feel so much better this morning! I kept off Facebook yesterday (Monday) and focused on my writing. Fran and I did some work together including further emails to TSA. We also looked at the hot springs she's hoping to visit at some point. Later on, we went on another walk around Ajijic. Fran seems very confident navigating the town. She put Glympse on so I could track where we were. It was fun to follow our progress on the map whilst simultaneously seeing what was going on via our video call. I know there are other parts of the town Fran would like to share with me. I hope so, because it was a lot of fun!

The only scary moment was when we crossed one incredibly busy road. I confess I held my breath as we dashed across, the cars seemed to flash by so fast! After our hiccup the day before, it was a great example of how it's possible to move forward without carrying grievances and issues along with you.

Overnight I had an email from a great friend of ours; best-selling author Julie A. Fast. She mentioned an exciting new writing opportunity but having seen my Facebook post, wondered if I might needed time before taking it any further. I so appreciated her consideration. I wrote back and said no, I'm good. This short break isn't about turning away people or opportunities that resonate with me. It's about paying attention to my boundaries so I can focus my energies where they can do the most good.

And that feels very healthy indeed.

[MB]

Our Mexican Adventure, Part Three: "Did We Just Buy a Condo?"

Posted February 7, 2018

THIS POST COVERS Fran's second week in the town of Ajijic in the State of Jalisco, on the north shore of Lake Chapala, Mexico.

Wednesday, 31 January 2018, 7:30 a.m. UK time
Fran and I had a brilliant Skype video call yesterday (Tuesday) at a café called Black and White in the Plaza. Fran propped her phone up on the table so I could see what was going on while we talked. It wasn't too busy and no one took the slightest notice. We were careful not to have the volume up too high. After a while, Fran saw someone she knew and called her over: a lovely lady called Paula from "the other Portland" (the one in Oregon!) The three of us nattered away as though we'd all known each other for years. Paula seemed amused and delighted that I felt so fully present with them there. Fran asked Paula about the "Super Blue Blood Moon" happening today (Wednesday), but the 6 a.m. meet up at the lakeside was just too early for Fran to contemplate! They plan to meet up on Thursday, though, to visit the hot springs which are a short bus ride away.

Thursday, 1 February 2018, 7:25 a.m. UK time
Fran visited the Black and White café again yesterday (Wednesday). She is great at connecting with new people she meets on vacation. ("I do better with strangers than

friends.") Later, she messaged me: "Hanging out with friends," and "had a deep deep talk with one lady."

We managed a short video call as I walked to the Metro station for the train after work. It was fun to show Fran the route I walk every day.

My evening was busy and satisfying. I watched a TV programme about the influence of the moon on life on earth (likely scheduled because of the Super Moon thing) and chatted online with a couple of friends. Later, I found some great music tracks on YouTube and made a decent start on a new piece of writing; about our book, suicide and suicidal thinking. It was about one in the morning when I went to bed.

The final message of the day from Fran: "Pizza! I've tried to come here for days! Finally it's open!"

Friday, 2 February 2018, 7:25 a.m. UK time

Fran went to the hot springs at Hotel Balneario yesterday (Thursday). It didn't exactly go to plan. She headed out to catch the bus, but despite asking several people if she was in the right place none of the buses stopped for her. She got more and more frustrated and cross with herself for not having walked to meet her friends and travel with them. ("I did plan it with them but nothing worked except them getting there and me not.") I suggested she tried Uber but she didn't want to do that. In the end she messaged one of her friends who told her she needed to walk about a mile along the road if she wanted to catch the bus. She headed off. A little later:

"On stupid bus."

"Put stupid Glympse on so I can see where you are. Do we know where we are going?"

Fran showed me the leaflet. I located the place on Google Maps and sent her screenshots to show where she needed to be, whilst simultaneously tracking her on Glympse. A nice lady on the bus helped by telling Fran where to get off. Finally she was there, and met up with her friends. She had a good time, and got a ride home, just missing a torrential downpour. We had a thirty minute call when she got back. She was cold, hungry, and grumpy.

"Shivering under the covers. I hope I don't get sick."

"Any headaches today?"

"No. Just shivering."

She seemed pretty low: understandable after the day she'd had. It took a while for her to fully engage with me, but after a bit we settled into our usual way of being with each other, and talked more readily. She is enjoying making new friends. She has invitations to dinner today (Friday), and tomorrow (Saturday). After we finished our call and she'd rested a while she headed out again, this time to a friend's birthday celebration. ("With cake!")

Thursday was #TimeToTalkDay here in the UK and I wore my Time to Change t-shirt into work. I was back on Facebook after my little break, and had a good conversation on one of my posts about the value (or otherwise) of awareness events like this. At work, I had three mental health related conversations. That's not at all unusual, actually: testament partly to the "looking out for each other" ethos my boss Judith engenders in her team.

Friday, 2 February 2018, 10:30 p.m. UK time

Fran's been busy today (Friday), including a tour round some local properties with a realtor (estate agent) which she arranged the other day. I messaged her when she got back.

"Did we just buy a condo?"

"Nope, but she was nice."

Right now, she's at Isabella's restaurant meeting friends for dinner. I doubt we will have any calls until tomorrow. I could have done with a natter, but it's okay. My day has been full, and heavy. I've been wrestling with one long-term friendship for a while and it kind of came to a head today. One in which I have struggled to accept the reality that I am not meeting my friend's support needs, and our relationship is not meeting my needs either. Not a failure, but a reminder that caring for someone isn't always enough, and that we need to keep an eye on our own well-being as well as the other person's.

On a more positive note, I received a lovely message from a lady thanking me and Fran for writing our book, which she was ordering to help her friend better support her. And then, tonight, a major new opportunity in the mental health arena presented itself (thanks, Julie!)

Saturday, 3 February 2018, 6 p.m. UK time

I have been out most of today (Saturday) with my family for my son Michael's birthday meal. Mike is a fantasy novelist, blogger, and cartographer. Fran has also been out, first for brunch and now visiting some gardens. She posted up a gorgeous sunset photo last night from down by the lake. Unfortunately, things didn't go so well as she made her way home.

"Please don't worry. I fell on my face walking home last night. I sent a piccie. I should have stuck with my beers. I had margaritas and egg nog. I don't remember falling on my face, but I do remember someone watching over me. The good thing is, I broke no teeth or leg or eye."

The photo showed some dried blood, minor cuts and scrapes on her nose and upper lip. I'm hoping it won't look too bad once she has cleaned herself up. But it will be sore and I know she will be concerned that she let it happen. The roads are pretty uneven and cobbled. That might be how it happened, although if she had been drinking too much that likely contributed too. I just have to trust that she's okay.

"Steve said it was the margaritas, and now I have my margarita story."

"Yeah. I was wondering if I'd have anything interesting for this week's blog …"

"My friends are concerned about me."

"I am too, Fran."

"I know."

We may not get to have a call or even chat much more today, as she is invited to dinner later with some other friends. There are times when the miles between us matter very little. And there are times like this.

Sunday, 4 February 2018, 1:10 p.m. UK time
Fran rested in the afternoon yesterday (Saturday) after her trip out for brunch/gardens. We got to catch up on chat later, before she went out for dinner with her friend Helen. She is planning a resting day today (Sunday), and wants to work on her photos and finances. She plans to watch tonight's Super Bowl if possible. I found an iPhone

app (Televista Deportes) which might work, if she decides not to go out anywhere to see it. We'll see. I'm hoping we will connect for a call at some point.

She sent another selfie: she has a cut to her upper lip and a Band-Aid across the bridge of her nose, but she managed a smile and I don't think there will be too much bruising, nor a black eye.

"I've had more things happen here in the last two weeks than I've had in the past year."

"How do you feel about that?"

"Probably shouldn't move here."

Monday, 5 February 2018, 7:30 p.m. UK time
I enjoyed yesterday (Sunday). I cooked lunch for my wife and son, went out for coffee and a few groceries, and spent the afternoon watching *Columbo*. I also chatted online a bit with a couple of friends. It's good to have people you feel comfortable and safe with, to share whatever might be going on for you without being judged.

I feel fully "caught up" again with Fran. We had a couple of voice calls through the day. We did a bit of "work:" we selected ten of her photos from the past week, emailed them out to her "postcard from Mexico" mailing list, and also posted them on Facebook. Best of all, we watched the Super Bowl! Fran hadn't wanted to go out anywhere and there wasn't a TV available to watch it on in the apartment.

After exploring a few options we found the best way was for me to have the game playing on my PC on the BBC Sport website. I then shared my screen with Fran via Skype. It meant we could be together on webcam and watch/hear the game at the same time. The picture was a bit "watercolour-y" at Fran's end. I pointed out it was probably easier to watch than in previous years, when Fran shared the Super Bowl experience with me by pointing her webcam across her apartment at her tiny TV!

Tuesday, 6 February 2018, 7:30 p.m. UK time
I focused my energies yesterday (Monday) on my writing and blogging, and replied to a very exciting email regarding a new opportunity in the mental health arena. Fran was really tired when we met on Skype last night (early evening for her). She is allowed to be tired of course, but it felt more than that. When I notice something that could potentially be more than it seems, I bring it into the open. Sometimes Fran will want to explore it, sometimes not. Last night, not.

"I know you're really tired, Fran, but you also seem — flat, maybe?"

"I am flat."

Instead, we talked about what's coming up in the next few days and I read more from *Outlander*, the novel we are reading together. After our call, Fran had an invitation to watch a movie with friends, but decided to stay in and rest until bed time. We're just over half-way through this trip. Later today (Tuesday) Fran will move from this apartment to another one nearby, where she will stay for the remainder of the trip. Tomorrow she has her first appointment at Dental Express, which is what started all this in the first place.

It's been quite an experience so far. Full. Exciting. Moving. Challenging. Painful, especially for Fran's nose. I can't wait to find out what happens next!

[MB]

Our Mexican Adventure, Part Four: Far in Miles, Close in Heart and Care

Posted February 14, 2018

THIS POST COVERS Fran's third week in the town of Ajijic in the State of Jalisco, on the north shore of Lake Chapala, Mexico.

Wednesday, 7 February 2018, 7:30 a.m. UK time
Fran still has a Band-Aid across her nose from the fall she took the other day, but her other injuries seem much healed. Mood-wise, she also appears less drained/down, which bodes well for today, when she has her first dental appointment. Fingers crossed that goes smoothly.

We had two calls yesterday (Tuesday). The first was sitting on a bench down by the lake; the second as she packed for her move to the new apartment where she will stay for the remainder of the trip. A friend helped her move. There was a message for me when I woke this morning to let me know she got there fine.

Thursday, 8 February 2018, 7:30 a.m. UK time
The first day of Fran's dental work went well yesterday (Wednesday), with fillings to one side of her mouth. The other side will be done on Monday. The periodontal (gum) work will be today (Thursday).

I was surprised Fran was able to talk and eat more or less normally afterwards. We met for a while when she was chilling out in a café after the procedure, and later had a lovely two hour call, back at her new apartment. Fran took me on a tour of the place but mostly we sat and talked. It was the best call we've here and the conversation ranged widely. I held space for Fran to share her stuff, and I got to share mine. I felt listened to, valued, and safe.

Friday, 9 February 2018, 7:35 a.m. UK time
Fran had a very full day yesterday (Thursday) with her periodontal surgery appointment at 11 her time. We chatted a little beforehand when she went for coffee, and afterwards as she went off to find the pharmacy to get her meds. That was a 25 minute walk along the very busy main road. I helped her find an alternative route that wouldn't be quite so busy. The surgery itself went well, and she didn't seem in too much pain or discomfort when we met again later back at the apartment. She wasn't up for doing too much of the talking, and I got to share some of the details from my day. That included the Mental Health First Aid course at work next month which my lovely boss Judith is keen I should attend. I'd love to, if there are places available.

While we were on our call, there was big thunderstorm, which Fran LOVED! I couldn't see the flashes of lightning but I could tell them from Fran's reaction, and soon learned to pause whatever we were talking about. I felt a strong flash of frustration when Fran told me she needed to stop our conversation so she could experience the present (Mexico) moment to the full, but we handled it well. She was clear about her needs, and my frustration at being "set aside" in favour of a thunderstorm passed as easily as the storm itself eventually did. And I got to experience it too: the sounds of thunder and rain, and Fran's delighted, awestruck response. Moments like this are what friendship is about.

Saturday, 10 February 2018, 10:15 a.m. UK time
Yesterday (Friday) was a quiet day for Fran in Ajijic, and a busy day for me in the office here in Newcastle! We had a good chat early evening when Fran was out at a restaurant. Our conversation is summarised by something she posted up on Facebook:

> Since I have been in Mexico I have taken most of my meals on my own. The beauty of this is that I can truly take in the Mexican food, decorations, and music, noticing what would not be noticed if I had company, and connecting with the servers to the point where they know my name. And I get to share my experiences with Marty, who is always with me even though he is across the sea. It's great to have a bestest friend!

We looked up how far apart we are geographically. It hadn't occurred to me that it's so much more than the usual 3,000 miles, It came back as 8,878 km, which is 5,515 miles! Fran posted that on Facebook too. A friend of ours, Judy, commented: "Interesting! Far in miles, close in heart and care." That meant a lot because not everyone gets it about distance friendships. Fran was really tired by the time we got together later, but we had an hour or so on Skype. I read from *Outlander*, and we talked about suicidality.

Sunday, 11 February 2018, 1:15 p.m. UK time
We had another good video call yesterday (Saturday) afternoon, when I was at the Costa coffee shop at Blackwell's Books in town. We talked about how she's

been feeling during this trip and about life generally. We continued the theme when we met in the evening, sat together on a bench at the lake side. Fran pointed out a heron. They must be common here because she's mentioned them a few times. There was also a heron on one of the murals she showed me the other day.

Fran's mood has definitely dropped. Depression? Perhaps, although it seems more a natural response to her feelings and thoughts about the trip, and whether she will be up to major travel like this in the future. Is that dream up for her? In part, Mexico was to see how she'd handle a trip like this on her own. I feel she's done remarkably well, but Fran doesn't see it that way. There are things she might do and places she might go, if she had more confidence, or someone to do things with. The bus ride experience put her off trying again. Her fall shook her more than I realised at the time. Typically, I focused more on the physical side of things — the cuts and scrapes — and didn't factor in how much it shook her self-confidence. That oh-so-busy main street is an issue too, because of the actual danger involved in crossing it, but also because of the impulses it engenders.

Later, Fran showed me a listing of local events that are on this coming week. Our final week in Mexico. I'm not sure if she'll want to take any of those up. I hope so. But she did go out with a friend for dinner last night (Saturday night). She just messaged me. "Had a nice time and a nice dinner last night. Great conversations. Thought-provoking." I'm so glad! Awkwardness and uncertainty in relationships disconcert her and leave her wondering if it's her fault. Congenial company is exactly what she needs: to connect with people and feel valued and welcome. Isn't that what we all want?

Monday, 12 February 2018, 7:30 a.m. UK time

On our call early evening yesterday (Sunday), I was delighted to hear what a great time Fran had had the previous evening. The good conversation, and the opportunity to just be herself, seems to have made a big difference. She told me, "Generally I think I have fragile self-worth." Well, things like this help reset that perception. Later, she was invited to a local Mexican lady's 21st birthday party. I've not heard yet how that went but I'm hoping and expecting she had a good time. Later today, she will be back at the dentist for her final work, apart from a final check-up appointment on Thursday. I spent my Sunday evening working on the new piece for the STOP Suicide website (it takes me so long to write anything!) and this week's Mexico blog, which I will start putting together tonight.

Tuesday, 13 February 2018, 7:30 a.m. UK time

I didn't get to see Fran yesterday (Monday), but we did chat on and off through the day. Amongst other things, we touched on her other friendships and mine: those that work and those that don't so well.

"Why do I keep getting hung up on the people and relationships where it's hard, or where things break down? It's okay, Fran, I'm just journaling my thoughts here."

"I always do this too."

"Yeah, I was thinking that. The parallels between us and our hang-ups."

"I'm always trying to win people over. It's part of my self-esteem project."

"I never feel I live up to other people's expectations of me. I think I try too hard. Or maybe people expect too much. The relationships that work for me are where I feel at ease to say my stuff, and the other person does too. Where I am not afraid to speak up."

Fran's dental work went well, although she needs one further procedure ("I need a crown! My first!") which will be done on Thursday. She also had a hearing test and has arranged a massage session for tomorrow, so she's clearly decided to make the most of her final week in Mexico. In the evening I focused on my writing. I got the Mexico blog ready to go up, apart from this entry I am writing now which I will type up tonight. I also completed, bar final edits and proof-reading, my piece for the STOP Suicide website.

Usually, I am keen for Fran to get back from her trips, but I'd be happy to stay here a bit longer.

"I'm going to miss Ajijic, Fran."

"Me, too."

There are still five days left: plenty of time for lots to happen. That's the thing, traveling with Fran, you never quite know what is around the corner. It's never boring!

[MB]

Our Mexican Adventure, Part Five: It's What We Do

THIS FIFTH POST covers Fran's final week in the town of Ajijic in the State of Jalisco, on the north shore of Lake Chapala, Mexico.

Wednesday, 14 February 2018, 7:30 a.m. UK time
Yesterday (Tuesday) was Shrove Tuesday here in the UK, and Mardi Gras Carnival in Mexico. Fran went out in Ajijic and found a great spot to watch the parade and festivities. She talked with local folk, including the children of one family who were sitting close by. It wasn't a situation Fran feels comfortable in ("I hate parades. I hate crowds. But this is as close as I'll get to Mardi Gras."), but she wanted the experience. And it certainly was an experience! People, colour, noise — and lots of flour!

"Me and my stuff are covered. Dammit. How can anyone think this is fun? It's in my phone, hair, purse, shoes, jacket, etc. But I made some nice connections. I'm finally using my iTranslate app to talk to people!"

We caught up properly back at her apartment, after she'd had a hot shower and washed out all the flour. We were on for a couple of hours and were able to properly catch up on what's been going on for each of us. We sat on the veranda, shared a beer, and took in the evening. I also got to meet Felix and Don who own the place. I really loved Felix's NYC shirt! Seeing and hearing how Fran interacts with the people around her, especially those she connects well with, helps me "place" her better in her environment and get a better handle on how she is doing. It's also a lot of fun for me!

Thursday, 15 February 2018, 7:30 a.m. UK time
We didn't get to have any Skype calls yesterday (Wednesday). I was really busy at work and Fran had a full day too. After her massage session, she went with a friend to the hot springs.

"Just finished hot tubs: Vinegar. Flowers. Magnesium. Coffee. Wine. Mud."

I can't wait to hear about it all!

Friday, 16 February 2018, 7:30 a.m. UK time
Fran went for what was supposed to be her final dental appointment yesterday (Thursday) but it turns out they couldn't do the crowns, so she will go back on Saturday. Other than that, it went well. We had two or three short calls in the evening. There were a few technical difficulties, but we stayed calm and tried again later. I was able to catch Fran up on some of what has been going on for me here. She isn't allowed solid food now until her crowns are done. She invited me to join her. So today (Friday), I'll not have any solid food until dinner this evening.

Other than that, I followed up on the new blogging opportunity I mentioned the other day. It sounds really exciting if it comes off. I also asked Laura Marchildon who runs the Our Bipolar Family website if she would like to review our book. (Thanks, Laura!) It feels good, in the midst of other stuff that is going on for me right now, to be progressing things in our mental health work. I took some me-time too, including time away from the PC. I also did a Loving Kindness meditation for the first time in ages. It helped, on a number of levels.

Saturday, 17 February 2018, 10:30 a.m. UK time
I'm sitting at a corner table in Porter's café in Tynemouth, beneath a big poster of the US flag. I'm maintaining my partial fast in support of Fran, which is a real pity because they have some amazing cakes and tray-bakes here, not to mention porridge! On the other hand, my weight dropped 2 lbs yesterday after my first day of partial fasting, so that's something!

Fran struggled quite a bit yesterday with not being able to eat. She made up for it with plenty of liquids, including a margarita in the afternoon and a large glass of red wine when we met on Skype in the evening. It's fair to say she was a bit tiddly! She'd had a grand day out, though, visiting the island fort of Mezcala on Lake Chapala. She posted a great photo on Facebook from the fort. She was really sleepy from her day out and drinking on an otherwise empty stomach. After talking for a little while she went for a lie down and fell asleep to me reading from *Outlander*.

We may or may not get to have a call tonight (Saturday night), but if not, last evening's call was a great way to round out our shared trip to Mexico. We've stayed in touch well, and if there have been times when I've gotten irritable and grumpy (which there have!), or Fran has (ditto!) then we have moved through them easily.

Last night Fran said she hoped I wasn't cross she'd been less present for me, with being away. It's true that I've had stuff going on, and had Fran been at home I probably would have explored it with her more than I've been able to. But she has been there for me, more than on previous trips in fact, and has been very supportive. And I've been blessed to find caring support in other places. (You know who you are. Thank you.)

I've used my Wellness Plan (today's trip to Tynemouth and the coast is a part of my self-care strategy) and moved through things as they have come up. I am proud of how Fran and I have each handled things.

Sunday, 18 February 2018, 10:25 a.m. UK time
I really enjoyed my day at the coast yesterday (Saturday). It gave me space to think, and not think. A pause in the pace and intensity of this past week or so. Fran's dental work, her four crowns, went well. ("Done. I've been crowned!") Afterwards, she met up with a friend for a meal of filet mignon and mashed potatoes at Los Telares.

I wasn't at all sure we would get to talk, but she called me as she walked back to the apartment from the restaurant. Voice only, but it was good to hear in person how she was feeling after the dental work, and at the end of her time in Ajijic. I also got the, now familiar to me, sounds of the town. Kids playing in the street. Snatches of Spanish from people as we passed by. And the dreadfully busy street Fran has christened "Butchers' Boulevard." I was genuinely relieved to make it safely across! I walked Fran back to the apartment, then said goodnight. It was close to one in the morning here in the UK, 7 p.m. in Mexico.

Today Fran will finish packing. She has a ride booked from Ajijic to the airport at Guadalajara. Then three flights and a bus ride home. Houston. Chicago. Boston. Portland. I will keep an eye on things for any delays or other changes. Hopefully it will be more straightforward than it was on the way out. As I posted on Fran's Facebook wall, "Safe and sure on your journey home!"

Monday, 19 February 2018, 7:35 a.m. UK time
Well, things didn't exactly go according to plan yesterday (Sunday)! The flight from Guadalajara to Houston went fine, but there were delays with the flight to Chicago which threatened her final connection. So … Plan B! Fran rearranged her tickets so she would overnight at the airport and catch an early direct flight to Boston. I updated the flights in my calendar, and the details I'd stored in my United Airways and Flight Hero apps so I could keep an eye on any delays. We checked to see if her bus ticket from Boston to Portland would still be valid (it would). It looked workable, apart from the fourteen or so hours Fran would have to spend at the airport.

"You can't drink beer all night!"

"I won't!"

Then Fran saw there was a better way. Plan C! More rearrangements and updates, but there was a flight from Houston to Newark within the hour, arriving just after midnight local time. That's where she is now. Her final flight, to Boston, is scheduled for 6 a.m. her time (my 11 a.m., we are back to five hours apart again — yay!) So, still quite a wait for her, but the end is in sight.

Traveling long distances like this is mentally and physically brutal, but once she is home later today there's not a lot she needs to do for at least a couple of days. R&R is definitely in order!

Tuesday, 20 February 2018, 7:30 a.m. UK time

I wrote yesterday (Monday) morning that travel can be brutal for Fran, physically and mentally, and this journey home from Mexico has certainly been that. She caught her final flight from Newark to Boston fine, but it was a scramble to make her bus connection.

"Welcome to Boston, Fran!"

"On plane. Stopped on runway. Hope we move fast. I really really want to get that bus but we're not moving. God damn. I am so sick of everything going wrong for me. I won't make it."

"It was always going to be close, but I did think we would make the bus."

"Those two hours until the next bus are gonna kill me."

"It might be delayed departing. When you do get off, you need exit door B115. The bus stop is right outside."

We did make the bus, just, but Fran had no time to look for her luggage. It turned out her suitcase was in Chicago anyway. Fran arranged for it to be sent on. I think it was delivered to her late evening. The two hour journey passed without incident ("Yay Maine. The bus was comfortable.") and a friend met Fran and drove her back to her apartment, stopping off for groceries on the way. Fran was finally home. I was expecting exhaustion but Fran also had bad neck pain, a headache and nausea which progressed to vomiting. I encouraged her to stay hydrated but she could keep nothing down.

"I'm wasted. My head is pounding. My neck is killing me. When will it stop."

"Did you get any sleep at all, overnight or today?"

"Spotty. I won't Skype at 2. Maybe 6 for a little bit."

"That's fine, Fran. You in bed?"

"On couch."

"Bed might be better for your back/neck."

Twenty minutes later: "I'm in bed." We Skyped at 6 p.m. (my 11 p.m.) but not for long. I left her to rest, but we chatted on and off for a couple of hours.

"I feel so sick I'm crying. Headache. Neck ache. Shivering. Nauseous."

"I didn't realise it was this bad. Just so I'm sure, you did take your regular meds yesterday/today with all the traveling?"

"Yes."

"Thanks. You're doing the right things. Do we need to think about seeing if someone can come sit with you?"

"Hold my hair."

"Holding it back."

"I'm so glad I am home dealing with this rather than traveling."

"Omg, yes. This would have been a nightmare overnight at the airport."

It was getting late.

"I'm going to bed. How are you feeling now? Still being sick?"

"A little better. I hope to sleep now."

There were no further messages overnight so, fingers crossed, Fran is sleeping. She doesn't need to be up early, or leave the apartment today. Extreme self-care. Back to basics. Pick up gently with things over the next few days. We will keep a watchful eye on her state of being as she emerges from this crash fatigue. There will be time enough to look back over the past four weeks in Mexico. Unpack. Sort through photos. Engage, gradually, with friends both at home and online.

And, no doubt, there will be other trips to think about, though we don't have any planned for this year. Travel is in Fran's bones, and I will support her as best I can. I will be here for her, as she is here for me.

It's what we do.

[MB]

Welcoming Myself Home

Published March 4, 2018

WHEN I AM DEPRESSED, I yawn a lot. It's as if I can't take a breath or don't want to. I sleep a lot and can't wake up. And it takes forever to do one task, if it indeed gets done. I just spent a month in Mexico where I pushed all my thoughts aside and intensely lived in the moment. Many things were wonderful, some not so much. Living alongside bipolar is not an easy thing to do, especially when traveling. Coming home I began unravelling and everything stopped. I was really sick in body and mind. I second guessed everything. The only thing I hung onto was that I was really proud of myself to do such an amazing thing. There are those who don't understand. I try to stay away from them. Understanding friends I cling to for they help me integrate in a healthy way. I continue to welcome myself home.

[FH]

The Most Anguishing Dilemma

Published March 28, 2018

THE MOST ANGUISHING dilemma with chronic illness is when you want to stretch yourself to do something you love, but you know it will challenge your health. A part of you hopes all will be well, hopes maybe you're getting better, hopes this time you can leave your cage behind. So you do the thing. And like clockwork the giant rubber band slaps and snaps and zaps you back further behind than you were before. Going to the doctor doesn't help. No answers there. Drugs can't touch it. There is only the quiet endurance of rest for as long as it takes to regain some ground and pray your mind doesn't go beforehand. And that your friends don't leave.

[FH]

Schrödinger's Fishing Tackle Box

Published April 21, 2018

WALKING INTO WORK this morning I found myself thinking about my mother's house which was cleared and sold last year. A few weeks ago I came across the property listing online, together with photographs of the house cleared for sale. Every room empty, including what used to be my bedroom. The first space in the world I could call my own. Walls stripped of wallpaper and painted an aseptic white. Floors clear and sanded. No trace of the home I knew. The décor and furnishings now live only in my memory and a few photos from past visits.

I'd suspected for some time that it wouldn't be long until the house was sold, if it was not already, to cover the cost of my mother's final years in nursing care. I could have asked someone about it, but was content to explore the uncertainty. Looking back on it this morning I smiled to myself, recognising it as a Schrödinger experience.

Unless or until I asked, the house, my home from birth until the age of eighteen when I left for university, was simultaneously sold and not. Curiosity may have killed the cat, but Erwin Schrödinger's feline remains alive and not-alive until someone looks inside the box and the entangled, quantum superposition states of live cat / dead cat collapse.

At my mother's funeral I was told — without my having asked and without anyone asking if I wanted to know — that the house had, indeed, been sold. But it was finding the photos online that collapsed the states for me. I looked inside the box. And found that the cat, or rather the home I had known for so long, was not dead. It simply was not. It no longer existed. Like my mother. Like my father, years before. Not.

And my mind turned to the things the house once contained. The furniture, books, LP records, clothes. Had any of these now not-things been mine? It seemed plausible, although if there were still items of mine in that house decades after my leaving home, how important to me could they have been? I mentally ticked off a list of things I knew I had rescued and brought up north over the years.

A wooden tractor and trailer my father made for me one Christmas. A wooden fort with drawbridge and moat, also my father's work. My collection of Action Man figures, uniforms, and equipment, including clothes my mother sewed and knitted by hand.

Another list, of things I was pretty sure I had never rescued and which were likely now *not*. Childhood board games. The six foot wingspan balsa wood glider I spend one summer building, filling my bedroom with balsa shavings, dust, and the rich aroma of cellulose dope. My scarcely used fishing rods.

And then I saw it in my mind's eye, in all its classic red painted glory. The wooden fishing tackle box my father made for me: another Christmas present, or possibly a birthday. I would have been in my teens, maybe 13 or 14.

I was never very into the fishing itself. I can't remember ever catching anything, despite visits to the canal with my cousin and to various park lakes with friends. But for a time I loved the craft and lore of it. I pored over angling magazines, crafted floats and lures from balsa wood, feathers, bits cut from tin cans, whatever I could lay my hands on.

I can see my tackle box now, clear as anything. The handle on the lid. The brass fastenings. I slide them open and lift the lid. Inside are all the floats, hooks, lines, lures and other paraphernalia. The scent of aniseed ground bait. And I wonder where that box is now. I'm not sure to which list it belongs. I may have brought it north at some point, in which case it is probably up in the loft. Or not.

It exists / not-exists. Like so much else. And I find I am okay with that, with the unknowningness.

Old Schrödinger was really on to something.

[MB]

Team Gum: How Fran and I Share Our Mental Health Journey

Published May 9, 2018

"You're stuck with me now, Frannie. I hope
you realise that."
"Like gum on my shoe."

FRAN AND I are a team. Team Gum. That's the starting point for pretty much everything we do, especially in the mental health arena. Our book. Our blog. Our social media presence. Podcasts. Interviews. Events. Book readings. Everything.

There are no hard and fast rules for how we balance things between the two of us and the many other aspects of our lives. It depends on the nature of the work itself, our individual skills, experience, and preferences. It also depends on our commitments, health, and whatever else may be going on at the time. I thought it would be interesting to take a look at how it all works for us.

Mental Health Experience and Awareness

It is no secret that before I met Fran I had little knowledge or awareness of mental health. Fran had a lifetime's worth, which she shared, and continues to share, openly and honestly. Mania. Depression. Suicidality. Fatigue. Pain. Insomnia. The realities of living with chronic mental and physical health conditions.

I learned from what Fran told me and by spending time with her every day. I also learned from the books I started reading, from courses and workshops, and by engaging with others. None of this means I really understand what it means to live with mental illness, but I do believe it helps me set Fran's lived experience, and that of others, in a broader context. I have also grown first-hand experience as a friend and caregiver.

Technical Skills

Fran worked as a highly successful electrical engineer before illness struck. She is technically competent, which is a huge benefit given that we live three thousand miles apart and do everything together online.

I work in the technology services industry (but please don't ask me to troubleshoot your laptop or printer!) and have a fair measure of web, graphics, and computing experience. I love the technical side of running our social media, website, and blog. When either of us is away from home I take the lead in ensuring we can keep in touch.

Writing and Creativity

Fran is a far more natural of a writer than I am. She is also a keen and accomplished photographer. She took the portrait photographs for her book, *For the Love of Peaks: Island Portraits & Stories: A Collection*. On the other hand, Fran's creativity depends a great deal on her health, energy and focus. The effect of illness on her motivation to create, her ability to do so, and the nature of her output (her writing in particular) can be profound. This is something we describe in our book. It makes it hard for Fran to work steadily at a project over a prolonged period of time.

I am more methodical and structured when it comes to writing. These are valuable traits when working on a long-term project like a book, or committing to a blogging schedule as I recently have with *bpHope.com*, but they come at a price. I struggle to connect with the creative flow, not least because I tend to self-edit as I write. It is something I continue to work with. For example, I am currently experimenting with writing my blog posts out longhand in one of my Midori notebooks and typing them up later for editing.

Energy and Focus

Creativity aside, the tidal nature of Fran's symptoms means she does not always have energy or focus to devote to projects. I provide the more or less stable structure to our work, keeping things moving forward so that Fran can contribute as and when she is able. As much as possible, we schedule our work around Fran's health, allowing time in between for rest and recovery. At least, that's the theory. We don't always get it right.

In the months leading up to the publication of our book *High Tide, Low Tide: The Caring Friend's Guide to Bipolar Disorder*, we were working flat out with our publisher to get everything finished on time and to standard. I did most of the editing, but each chapter, indeed every sentence, was proofread several times by us both. Fran was heavily involved at every stage, including contract negotiations and book cover. She took a series of photographs, which contributed greatly to the concept development, although they weren't used in the final design.

We had an online cover reveal and a book launch, which was hosted online by both of us and in person by Fran. This was followed by a book reading and charity fundraiser at a venue in Portland, Maine. Almost all the physical work for that fell to Fran, and she hosted the event, with me attending virtually on a big screen at her side via the magic of the internet. In addition to all this we arranged interviews and podcasts, and there were marketing and promotion leads to be followed up on.

It was the culmination of four years' work. It was very rewarding, but also exhausting and frustrating. It led ultimately to Fran getting severely fatigued and sick. She needed a prolonged period afterwards to recuperate.

Mental Health Community

Early on, our mental health contacts were all on Fran's side of the Atlantic. Mostly these comprised her professional support team and people she had met over the years. As Fran's friend and caregiver, I got to know, and be known by, many of these people and organizations. Maine Health. It Takes A Community. NAMI Maine. Family Hope. Over time, we started connecting with mental health groups and individuals online. Many of these were also in the US, including Stigma Fighters and No Stigmas.

At some point, I recognized that I needed to up my game and connect with the mental health community here in the UK. My first approach was to Time to Change, the UK-wide charity campaigning to end the stigma and discrimination associated with mental illness. It was one of my wisest moves, and led to me connecting with many wonderful folk. Much of our outreach is done through social media, but I have taken up the opportunity to attend events here in the north-east of England and further afield, including speaking at a mental health event last year in Ely. For someone who used to have no social life and little in the way of social skills, it is a wonder and a delight to me that my life has changed so much.

It is interesting how our social skills complement each other. Fran is brilliant at meeting new people, which is helpful on vacations where she will strike up conversations with folk she has never met before. She finds it harder to maintain connections and friendships long-term. I have always felt more comfortable with established relationships, although I am learning to relish new connections and first time conversations. I have certainly come out of my shell to the extent that I now enjoy the people side of our work.

Visibility and Risk

Much of our motivation for working in the mental health area is to challenge stigma and discrimination, and to share the message that living with mental illness does not preclude or prevent deeply meaningful and mutually supportive relationships. The flip side of that coin is that stigma and discrimination really do exist and are rarely pretty. We risk negative reactions any and every time we raise our heads above the parapet. Every Facebook post, every open and honest conversation, may bring unwanted and unwarranted reaction.

The risk falls more on Fran's head than mine. She is the person living with illness. She is the one with the diagnoses, the one whose symptoms, behaviours, and situation are being described or explored. With very few exceptions, I have always felt listened to and supported when talking about our friendship, about our book and work together, and about other crisis events in my own life. Fran, on the other hand, has personal experience of harsh and stigmatising treatment at the hands of others, and we go out of our way to protect against that happening again. It is part of the reason I am more of the public face of Team Gum.

Commitment and Motivation

A few years ago, Fran and I spent some time coming up with vision and mission statements for our mental health work.

> VISION: Our vision is a world where no one is too far away to be cared for or to care.

> MISSION STATEMENT: To inspire connections between the ill and the well for a stronger more compassionate world.

Fran expresses her commitment with characteristic simplicity on her social media profile: "Passionate about making invisible illness visible."

I recently changed my Twitter handle to include the words: *Mental Health Author and Advocate*. This has brought me some negative feedback from people who see it as self-aggrandisement, or believe that I imagine I always know what to do or say to someone living with a mental health condition. Nothing could be further from the truth! I thought long and hard before claiming these labels. Doing so acknowledges how central our work has become to my sense of who I am and what I can contribute. No more, no less.

Just about everything I do or am involved in is part of our joint commitment to effect positive change. If I often take the lead it is because I have fewer challenges to face, not because I am more committed or passionate about what we are doing. I am encouraged and supported by Fran at every step. We bring different things to the party and complement each other well. It is fascinating to me to witness how we have grown and learned from and with each other over the almost seven years we've been friends.

[MB]

Tribe and Un-tribe (A Trip to the Pub)

Published May 26, 2018

ALMOST EXACTLY a year ago, I wrote about visiting Wylam Brewery Tap Room at the Palace of Arts in Exhibition Park, Newcastle. I returned today, and as I sit, (inside, because there's some sort of food festival going on outside in the beer garden) I am thinking back over the months that have passed since I was here last.

My wife Pam and I have enjoyed three vacations in Cumbria: a week last July in Bowness, a week in October just outside Brough, and a week this April in Appleby. Christmas was spent quietly at home. In March, we travelled down to Liverpool with our two adult children for my mother's funeral.

At work, I'm still doing the same job in the same place, which hasn't challenged me for quite some time. However, as of the past two weeks, I am feeling far more optimistic and engaged. She refuses to take any of the credit, but this is very much down to my brilliant boss Judith, with buy in and encouragement from senior management, all the way up to and including our Chief Exec.

It occurs to me this is the third Newcastle pub I have been in this month, which must be some sort of record! It's not the alcohol (though I would be hard pressed to fault the pint of Collingwood Pale Ale I'm drinking). Rather, it's a growing confidence in myself as someone who needn't feel out of place in a social setting. I am reminded of something I wrote some time ago.

Be aware of the stories we tell ourselves, especially those that begin "I'm not the kind of person who …"

Although I'm here on my own today, an important aspect of this is that I have people locally who are glad to see me, and places and events where we can meet. As I wrote recently, I have found my tribe. Of course, if there is a tribe there must be an un-tribe. Fran and I have been talking recently about the importance of boundaries and distinguishing healthy connections from unhealthy ones. About those people we recognise (and are recognised by) as "our people." Those we resonate with. Those we feel safe with and respected by.

This doesn't mean we get to ignore or behave badly towards people who are not our tribe. (I've come a long way from the days when I had an Inner Circle of "Special People," and I'm not going back there!) However, it does mean we get to respect our boundaries and decide where to focus our time and energy. There is a flipside, of course, which is that we may find ourselves on the outside of other people's boundaries. There will be people for whom our attention, attitudes, life choices etc. are fundamentally unhealthy. Even toxic. And that's okay too. Respect the other person. Respect yourself. And move on.

"I'm here. I'm me. I'm growing. I'm learning. I'm flawed. I mess up. I fess up. I love. I am loved. It is enough. I am enough."

Mine's a pint, by the way. Cheers!

[MB]

Frustration and Co-dependency: Getting It Wrong Is Okay

Posted June 13, 2018

WHEN FRAN AND I were developing the ideas for our book, I kept a series of "Scrapbook" documents. In them I recorded anything that occurred in our lives which seemed relevant and might prove useful or helpful. Excerpts from our conversations, social media chat, and emails; snippets from my personal journal; ideas and questions; links to websites, books, and other reference material. This post is taken from notes made in December 2012, with a few minor edits for clarity.

Thursday December 13, 2012

Last night at 11 p.m. I was waiting for Fran to get home and come online. She messaged me to say she was home and was going to send her friend a happy birthday message. I was happy to hear that and thought she wouldn't be long … then she messaged that she was going to check my Facebook Wall. I started to get impatient. I felt Fran could have come on cam with me while she did that. But I put on some gentle music and did some meditative breathing while I was waiting.

Fran came on webcam a little later, around 11:25 or 11:30, and the first thing she said was that she had found the "two minutes of calm" video I'd posted and had meditated to that (and in fact rather longer than two minutes). I did feel pissed off then, partly because I had thought Fran and I could have done that together. (We did, later, once I had regained my composure).

Part of me recognised that, of course, Fran was and is free to do whatever she wants to do before coming online to meet with me, and she'd been out all day and must have wanted and needed a little space to herself first … But another part of me was feeling aggrieved, thinking that she knew I was waiting for her and would be eager to see her. It was a classic pouty moment!

Of course, it didn't last too long! Fran was great with me and allowed me to feel what I was feeling, until I was ready to let go of it. THAT is why we work so well together. We understand how these things work. The day before she had been all uptight about not having heard back from one of her friends about accommodation for their trip to Barcelona and I gave her space to feel and express that so she was ready later to talk with her friend and get things sorted. That is what we do for each other.

All that led onto something else that is really important regarding our book.

Fran said the book needs to include difficulties the well one (caregiver) experiences as the ill one moves towards wellness: the shifts in role, the sense of abandonment. The sense that all this care has been given and what is the caregiver going to get back in return? It fit what had just happened: me feeling Fran should want to be with me as much as I wanted to be with her, whereas in fact she was taking care of herself and paying attention to what she needed in a very healthy way.

It also fit with my abandonment responses at different times, when Fran has wanted and needed to find her own space. We have plenty of examples to draw on! This is a really important topic. [MB]

Looking Back on a Productive and Positive Week

Posted June 20, 2018

Saturday, 16 June 2018

I AM AT Tynemouth Metro station this morning. The weekend market is relatively quiet so far. Bustle without the hustle. I have a large Americano from the excellent Regular Jo's coffee stall, and the table to myself. I've caught up with my diary and written to one of my oldest (ahem, longest-standing!) friends. It is time to open my Midori notebook and think about this week's blog post.

It has been a busy but very positive and fulfilling week for me on the mental health front. I spent an hour last evening editing the latest in a new series of articles by a great friend, renowned author and family coach Julie A. Fast. Julie's posts are always amongst the most popular on our site. This latest one focuses on managing paranoia.

Fran and I received several messages this week from people who have read or are reading our book, or have connected with us in other ways. We're not in the advice business but it means so much when our words resonate with others or if we have been able to shed a little light on someone else's situation. It sounds trite but that really is what it's all about for us.

And we gain so much in return. At the moment I am working on what will be my sixth article for *Bp Magazine*. My latest topic is the glamour (in the sense of enchantment) of euphoric mania. I am working from our own experience (as many of you know, Fran was in mania when we met back in 2011), but am also drawing on the experience of others who have shared with me and are happy to contribute. This kind of collaboration expands my knowledge and hopefully makes for a more rounded article. Fingers crossed on that score!

Speaking of collaboration, I am working with some fabulous people at the company where I work to get some new mental health initiatives off the ground. It is early days but we are beginning to pull some ideas together. It is hard to overstate how much it means to me and I am determined to make the most of the opportunity. It has already led to new connections and conversations, new training including a half-day session next week on neurodiversity and an excellent dial-in last week on resilience, as part of Carers' Week.

That I can do this at all is down to the support and encouragement of my boss Judith. When people care for those around them as much as she does, at work or in any other environment, anything is possible. That is the culture our newly formed mental health team is looking to foster. I drafted Vision and Mission Statements this week for us. They may be amended or someone may come up with something better altogether! But for me they capture the essence of what we are about.

> OUR VISION is a working environment in which we all feel safe, supported, valued and heard.

> OUR PURPOSE is to foster a workplace culture and practices free from mental health stigma and discrimination, by raising awareness of mental health conditions,

support services, events and organisations, encouraging relevant education and training including Mental Health First Aid (MHFA), and providing appropriate support to colleagues, including signposting to internal and external services.

Okay. I've just about finished my coffee. It's time to take a look round the market. Who knows what I might find. I am curious to find out. That's kind of what life's about, I think.

[MB]

Being Jimmy Perez: *Shetland* and the Art of Listening

Published June 27, 2018

Spoiler alert: this post touches on aspects of the British television crime drama Shetland.

FRAN AND I watch a lot of TV and movies together. Our talking done for the evening, Fran turns her laptop (and thus me) to face her television and we settle down to Netflix, a DVD, or occasionally a TV show.

We can see each other reflected in the screen: Fran on her couch and me in my desk chair. We might comment on what's going on or ask a question, but it's hard to hear each other unless Fran pauses the show. So for the most part we sit and watch — and listen — in companionable silence.

It sometimes feels like we do this a bit much. We used to talk more, sharing what had gone on for us that day or making plans for whatever was coming up. We still do that, of course, just less than we did. There are reasons for the change, not least the fact that Fran's fatigue has been especially hard on her this year. By the time we get together for an evening she is often too tired to talk much. But the other night as we watched the British detective drama *Shetland*, something fell into place for me about the value and importance of listening.

We both love the show: the stunning scenery, the gritty city environment of Glasgow, the accents, the superb writing and storylines. We've taken the characters very much into our hearts. Played by Douglas Henshall,

Detective Inspector Jimmy Perez is one of very few male roles I've ever identified with or wanted to emulate. This series has seen him navigate a range of personal challenges, most notably with his detective sergeant Alison "Tosh" Macintosh (played by Alison O'Donnell), his stepdaughter Cassie (Erin Armstrong), and Cassie's biological father Duncan (Mark Bonnar). Jimmy and Duncan have a close, awkward, almost brotherly relationship that is beautiful to watch.

What struck me is how good Perez is with people going through crisis and change. He is less good with his own crises and changes, but isn't that the way of things? (The series closes with a hint he may finally be finding a way forward.) Whether interviewing a suspect; talking with witnesses; confronting a violent crime boss; or engaging with colleagues, his stepdaughter, or a new lover, Jimmy Perez is usually calm and measured, although he can be assertive when necessary. He doesn't always get it right, but he owns his mistakes. He comes across as honest, genuine, and caring. He is someone you'd feel safe with.

It is this aspect of his character that most interests me. More and more I find myself in a listening role. I don't always know what to say, but I have learned that what matters most is showing up, being present, and being prepared to listen. It is good to see this demonstrated so clearly, even if it is in a fictional setting.

A friend said to me the other day, "The distinction between hearing and listening is important."

She's right. So often we imagine we have been listening to someone when really all we did was register the sounds they made. Listening is as much about the spaces between the words (and at the end of them) as it is about the words themselves. It is not as easy as it might seem.

At a meeting last week with our company's mental health team, I suggested setting up a small lending library. I have lots of relevant books at home and am more than happy to bring them in. One is Gail Evans' *Counselling Skills for Dummies: A Practical Guide to Becoming a Better Communicator and Listener*. It has lots of useful information, tips, and techniques. It is well worth checking out if you get chance. I might read it again before I take it in.

Genuine listening involves far more than letting someone talk. (Or write. Much of my listening takes place online using social media, instant messaging, and emails.) There are certain things not to do. Don't interrupt. Don't leap in with potential fixes or your own experiences. These get in the way and are rarely as relevant to the other person as you imagine. There are specific things you can do. Check in now and again to confirm you are picking up what the other person wants to convey. Ask for clarification if necessary. Encourage gently. If you want to know more, check out the Dummies book, or ours: *High Tide, Low Tide: The Caring Friend's Guide to Bipolar Disorder*.

Best of all, practice. That means engaging with your friends, colleagues, partner, children, strangers. We are all different and our needs are complex and wonderful. This was brought home to me on a neurodiversity workshop I attended recently at work. The course material was good but what I found most valuable was listening as the trainers and others in the group shared their experiences, and I shared mine. (I have just noticed I am wearing a

Stigma Fighters t-shirt today with the slogan "Sharing Our Stories.")

This is where the magic happens. We can aspire to no higher calling than to be someone others feel safe enough with to be vulnerable. Be like that. Be like Jimmy.

[MB]

No Promises Asked For, Offered, or Needed.
A Vacation Postcard to My Best Friend.

Published July 12, 2018

Monday, 9 July 2018

DEAR FRAN,

It is 7:10 p.m. here in the UK, and 2:10 p.m. with you in Maine. This hour is our hour. Usually we would be on Skype, catching up on our news and our plans. Just hanging out together, as friends do, no matter where they live or how far apart they might be.

This isn't a normal week, though, is it? I am on vacation here at Ambleside in the English Lake District. Travel — on either my part or yours — inevitably means some disruption to our routine. One Skype call per day instead of two, for example. Or shorter calls. Occasionally none. That used to hurt. These days not, or not so much. We have learned to trust.

We are doing okay so far this week! We had video calls on Saturday and Sunday evenings, down by the jetty opposite the fish and chip shop. It is always fun to be on a call with you when I am "out and about," able to not merely tell you what's going on for me but show you.

The lake here at Ambleside (technically, where we are staying is called Waterhead, but it is part of the town of Ambleside). The roar of motorbikes leaving the car park next to where we were sitting yesterday. Sadly, Skype doesn't yet permit the sharing of smells; I would so have liked to share with you the tangy aroma of exhaust fumes as one biker revved her Harley in my face! I showed you inside the Wateredge Inn, your first English pub. Maybe next time we will stay for a drink.

We touched a couple of times on chat earlier today to share our respective good mornings, and our weights. (At 185.2 lbs mine was close to the lowest it has been in many months, which is especially rewarding, given I'm on vacation, when good practice is harder to maintain.)

No call today, though. Whilst I am enjoying the peace and tranquillity of Borrans Park at the very northernmost point of Windermere (note I say tranquillity, not silence: I can hear the lapping of waves at the shoreline, the call of birds in the air and on the water, voices from the pub, traffic, and a troupe of teenagers making their way in a very orderly fashion through the park) — whilst I am enjoying all this and taking photos and writing these words to share it with you later, you are out with friends having adventures of your own!

All being well — no promises asked for, offered, or needed — we will have our call tomorrow evening. And then you are off on a mini vacation of your own to Monhegan Island! Four days. Three nights. No promises asked for, offered, or needed, we will do our best to connect. To share words, the sounds of our voices, video, photos, the essence of who and where we are in the moment.

Because the moment is what we have to share. It is all any of us have. Seven plus years of moments have brought us to here as best friends. A heap more will carry us wherever we are set to go. Calls or not, Fran, I will be with you when you are away. As you are with me here today.

Hah! You just messaged me: "Milkshake AND ice cream. On boat."

I figure you're having fun! It's not just that we are best friends, of course, is it? There is more to it than that. There is trust. And honesty. And vigilance. You messaged me earlier today: "Should I bring Risperdal? I wonder if I am bordering on mania."

I replied: "You mean today? Or for your trip? Definitely on the trip (it is on your packing list already). It is also worth bringing with you today if you are asking the question."

And so, at the mention of "milkshake AND ice cream," I remind you to keep an eye out for that edge of mania. And that is how we are. We can switch seamlessly from whatever it might be that we are doing or talking about, into a deep and yet simple caring awareness that works both ways. (Not everyone gets that — that you are here as much for me as I am for you. In different ways, perhaps, but no less.) Thank you.

See you soon.

Marty

[MB]

What a Week That Was!

Posted August 1, 2018

I'M WRITING THIS at AMT Coffee in Newcastle's Central Station. I am meeting a friend in an hour or so but right now it's Marty time. Just over a week ago I attended Newcastle Recovery College Collective's leaving party at Broadacre House. The college is moving to new accommodation in the autumn and there was a distinct end of an era feel about the event which amply demonstrated how important ReCoCo is to those who use it. I had a fabulous time listening to the karaoke and even got up to dance at one point. Thanks to everyone for making me feel so welcome.

The following day I volunteered for Time to Change at Newcastle Pride. This was the third time I'd done so and as usual I had a great time catching up with old friends and making new ones. We were there to engage with folk visiting the event, to share information and answer questions about Time to Change, and to help encourage a more open approach to mental health. I lost count of my conversations but one or two in particular left an impression on me. As I told a friend later:

> For me, what makes it so worthwhile is when I am talking to someone who might not be used to sharing about their mental health and I comment or ask a question and they are like "yes!" In that moment there is this really genuine human connection. That happened a few times today.

Monday was a big day for me. It was my debut appearance on the Executive Team call at work. I was there to present the mental health initiatives I've been helping develop with the rest of our fledgling mental health team. I'd got myself all stressy about the technology side of attending the call, but thanks to several colleagues especially my fab boss Judith, and Cheryl who let me impersonate her for the occasion, it all went smoothly. My main objective was to gain approval for the company to sign up to Time to Change's Employer Pledge Scheme. It says a lot about our leadership team that my recommendation was approved unanimously. I'm looking forward to taking things forward in the weeks to come.

Outside of work my week has been rich and full with phone calls and chats and face-to-face conversations with friends near and far. After a couple of weeks' break I've also got back to my writing, with a new article on bipolar anger. In something of a departure for me I have been able to draw on a wide range of experiences generously shared by others. It has broadened my knowledge and awareness and the final article will be far richer for it. Anger is a fascinating topic and I'm already considering a possible follow-up article.

So yes, it has been a busy week! I wonder what the next one will bring?!

[MB]

Even the Good Things: A Lesson in Letting Go

Published August 8, 2018

THERE ARE MOMENTS when everything stops.

I felt it yesterday after a week or more filled with activity and possibilities and new friends and old friends and a movie that touched me deeply.

After all of that, there came a pause. Not an ending, but a natural hiatus. Like the moment between breathing in and breathing out that we fail to notice most of the time because we are too busy doing or saying or thinking about other things. And I didn't know what to do with it. The gap. The space. I told Fran I felt flat, and she said:

"Embrace the flatness."

That was it. Three words. She knew I didn't need a lecture or a diagram or a two hour conversation. And she was right. And what came to me in that moment of being reminded was something we have been working with over the years we have been friends.

FEEL IT. CLAIM IT. LOVE IT. LET IT GO.

And so that's what I did. In this context, "Embrace" stood for the first three parts: Feel, Claim, Love. I felt what I had labelled as "flatness." I found that it was not empty or still at all. At its "flat" surface emotions rose and fell back, shifting in and out of existence even as I became aware of them. It was a dynamic emotional silence, like the kind of acoustic silence that is alive with ambient sound. I smiled.

140

I claimed it as mine. No one else was responsible or to blame. No one else in the history of the universe, past, present or future had known, or knew, or would know this moment as I had the capacity to know it. This was mine. This was me. I loved it. I was aware of a rush of love that began with me and expanded out to all my friends, my family, all the people in my life, all the events and connections between them and me and within them and between us all. A moment of acceptance. The kind that makes you sigh out loud.

And letting go? I recalled a poem I'd read aloud to Fran a few days before. It was titled *She Let Go*, by Safire Rose. It wasn't new to us, but some things are worth revisiting.

> Like a leaf falling from a tree, she just let go.
> There was no effort.
> There was no struggle.
> It wasn't good and it wasn't bad.
> It was what it was, and it is just that.

So I let go. I let go of my expectations of what flatness ought to be. I let go of any judgment about what I was feeling or not feeling or doing or not doing. I let go of my attachment to even this moment of bliss. And I smiled again, hearing a friend's words clearly in my mind: "Even the good things I've got to let go?" Not the things, but the feels, yes. How else can the next feelings arrive if you're holding on too tightly to the old ones? You don't have to let go of them immediately, just don't hold on too long. It's mostly the bad things we hold on to too long.

[MB]

Not to Punish but to Understand

Published August 15, 2018

SOMETIMES IT HAPPENS that you read or hear or experience something so sharp, so surprising, so out of left field, so TRUE that it stops you in your tracks. That's what happened the other day when I came across this quote on social media:

> Imagine meeting someone who wanted to learn your past not to punish you, but to understand how you needed to be loved.
> — Author unknown

There is personal relevance in the words for me and others in my life right now, but that's not what I want to write about. What I want to explore — and I am writing as much for me as for you, dear reader — is why it would ever be otherwise. Why are those lines so shocking? Ought not every person we meet, certainly every person we allow in close, approach us in such a way?

Perhaps. Well, yes in fact. But for a whole heap of reasons silence and stigma and shame remain powerful forces in society at large and in the smaller, more immediate communities in which we live out our lives. Wherever we meet — in our places of work and of worship — the response to us, to our stories and histories, so often falls short of the caring curiosity for which we yearn. Sadder still, we punish ourselves for what we have done or said, or failed to do or failed to say; the times we believe we have let ourselves or others down. How rarely do we approach ourselves with compassion?

What would it feel like if we did? How would it feel to explore our own stories wanting not to punish but to understand how we need to be loved?

[MB]

Let's Talk about Talking: Three Conversation Types for a Mutually Caring Relationship

Published September 4, 2018

I AM GRATEFUL to my friend Vikki Beat for our recent conversation at Caffé Nero, which led to me writing this up. It's no secret that Fran and I spend a lot of time talking together, but it took a while for me to recognize that not all conversations are the same. Different people have different ways of talking, of course, but aside from that there are distinct types of conversation, depending on what the people involved need at the time. Here are three distinct types we have found useful.

My Turn, Your Turn

This is the type of conversation that comes most naturally to me, whether face-to-face (in person or on a video call), on the telephone, or in online chat. It consists of short alternating exchanges, one person speaking for a moment or two then letting the other take a turn. It works well (at least for me) where you are "shooting the breeze," making plans, or sharing things on a fairly superficial level. What I had to learn is there are situations where it isn't necessarily appropriate or helpful.

It Will Be Your Turn in a Minute

The "my turn, your turn" approach doesn't work for Fran if she is trying to share something detailed or important. From her point of view, my wanting to speak every minute or so means I am constantly interrupting her train of thought. Once interrupted, she finds it next to impossible to pick up again. This was especially so early in our friendship when Fran was in mania. It was hard enough for her to slow her thoughts to a pace and order where she could share them with someone else. She needed me to let her speak for a while without interrupting. Then I could take my turn to comment on what she had shared, ask a question, or take things in a new direction. This felt very unnatural to me at first, and I still find it hard sometimes. But I've learned that slowing things down like this (essentially conversing in short monologues rather than exchanging sentences) can be incredibly valuable, whether you have difficulties marshalling your thoughts or not.

I Need to Talk

There are times when we want and need to just let the words flow, to "dump" (I hate that expression), to express whatever it is we are feeling or thinking without being interrupted, questioned, or judged. It is what Thich Nhat Hahn has called deep listening.

> Deep listening simply means listening with compassion. Even if the other person is full of wrong perceptions, discrimination, blaming, judging, and criticizing, you are still capable of sitting quietly and listening, without interrupting, without reacting. Because you know that if you can listen like that, the other person will feel enormous relief. You remember that you are listening with only one purpose in mind: to give the other person a chance to express themselves, because up until now no one has taken the time to listen.

This is important work and carries a degree of responsibility. As the listener, you may feel any number of things: pain, hurt, joy, pride, love, anger. You might yearn to interrupt with advice and suggestions. It's okay. You get to feel it all, and you get to keep it to yourself. Your input, suggestions, and opinion may be welcome later, but right now your role is to be wholly present, to STFU, and to listen. It is NOT easy. At least, I don't always find it so. Persevere. It is perhaps the greatest gift you can offer another human being.

Vikki and I joked how maybe we ought to make some flags we can hold up to let the other one know what type of conversation we want or need. That might be taking things a little too far (though it would be fun) but it is important in any relationship that both people can express what they need in the moment. As far as conversation types go, this can be as simple as holding up your hand to indicate you've not finished talking yet, or saying, "I need you to listen right now while I get all this out, okay?" Our ability to do this — and to accept that we still sometimes get it wrong — is why Fran and I work so well together.

When two people are open and honest with each other and come together to share words, space, and time, it can be a truly beautiful thing.

> Out beyond ideas of wrongdoing
> and rightdoing there is a field.
> I'll meet you there.
> — Rumi

[MB]

Follow Your Passion: A Merry Meeting

Posted September 19, 2018

I BUMPED INTO an old friend and former colleague this morning as I was having coffee at Regular Jo's at Tynemouth Market. The last time I saw Paul was in similar circumstances. He saw me one Sunday afternoon as I was sitting outside Starbucks near where I live. That was maybe eighteen months ago. I know our book *High Tide, Low Tide* was out.

It was great to see him again today and we had a good catch up, sharing what each of us is doing these days, and checking in on folk we know or knew. Paul left to follow his dream of working for himself at something he loves, and it is clear it's worked out well for him. That was great to see!

On paper at least I'm doing much the same work as I was doing the last time we met. (As a matter of fact I have been doing much the same work since Paul left, which might be ten years ago now.) But I am not the same person I was then, and I can honestly say I am much happier since I started help shape the mental health initiatives we have going on within the company.

At the moment this is only a minor aspect of my role, I remain primarily engaged in the "techie stuff" of applications support, but the mental health side has transformed how I feel about going to work each day. It is something I am passionate about and want to develop further, with the ongoing support of colleagues and management. I think that came across to Paul as we were talking. It's hard to hide the light inside when it burns so brightly, as Paul's did when talking about his work and life.

So, it was a merry meeting: each of us "living the dream" and looking ahead in hope to wherever our respective journeys might take us next. Not a bad way to spend a Saturday morning!

[MB]

What Newcastle Recovery College Means to Me

Posted October 3, 2018

NEWCASTLE RECOVERY COLLEGE COLLECTIVE (ReCoCo) is a joint venture between various organisations in the north east of England, "by and for service users and carers. [It is] a place where service users are able to make connections and develop their knowledge and skills in relation to recovery."

I first heard about ReCoCo through folk I've met volunteering with Time to Change. I was intrigued but hadn't taken it any further until July when my friend Vikki Beat invited me to attend the end of term party. The event also marked the college's relocation from Broadacre House to its new home just down the road in Anderson House. I didn't know many people at the party, but I felt very welcome. I even had a dance! I remember thinking it would be great to work more closely with the college in some way, but I couldn't see how that might work, as sessions are held during the week and I am in full time employment.

The college closed over the summer, but I was keen to check out the autumn prospectus as soon as it came out. For the past six months I've been working with a fantastic group of people where I work to promote mental health awareness and support within the company. I immediately saw how some of ReCoCo's courses were relevant to me personally and to our workplace initiatives. After discussing with my manager I phoned the college to make an appointment.

My enrolment interview was last week. Lynne explained the college's code of conduct and collected basic information from me, including any special needs or requirements I might have. She then led me through completing a Peer Support Empower Flower, which is "a self-reported measurement tool based on the principles of peer support." I found the exercise fascinating and (gently) challenging as I was encouraged to explore how I was feeling in eight categories: Feeling Connected, Recognising My Strengths, Feeling Hopeful, Taking Control, Taking Responsibility, Self Worth, Having Purpose, and Keeping Myself Safe. I left feeling very proud to be a student for the first time in many years!

I had arranged to meet Vikki after my enrolment, and she suggested we return to Anderson House for the afternoon drop-in session. I'm glad we did because it gave me the opportunity to meet some of the staff, volunteers, and other students. The atmosphere was warm, gentle, and compassionate. I felt welcome and accepted, and my contributions and story were considered as respectfully as anyone else's. (As someone without direct lived experience of mental illness, crisis, or trauma, it is a big thing for me to feel I have something worth sharing that might be of interest and value to others.) It left a powerful impression, as I wrote later to my workplace mentor:

> I had a great time at Newcastle Recovery College. I enrolled for the courses I want to do (a short session on self-harm next week, and then the Wellness Recovery Action Plan awareness course next month). A friend invited me to stay into the afternoon for the weekly drop in session. The difference the

college makes – that the staff and volunteers and students make – to the lives of the people who attend is simply staggering. It makes you question what you are doing with your life. Which is where you come in, of course; to help me find a way to do more of that here at work!

I asked Vikki, who is a volunteer and course facilitator at ReCoCo as well as being a student, if she would share what the Recovery College means to her.

I started coming to the Recovery College three years ago. At the time I was experiencing stigma first hand through my career within the NHS. The best way to describe the feeling of the Recovery College is that it's like a family. A family without judgment. And just like a family, we argue. And like a family we kiss and make up (not literally, of course!) Three years on and I am now a volunteer for ReCoCo and facilitate my own course. Watching nervous and anxious individuals come into the college and blossom into the confident people they become is awe-inspiring. We all struggle at times, but ReCoCo is a safe place to come and support each other. I'd like to thank all the staff and volunteers for being my solid rock.

I look forward to attending the first of the sessions I have enrolled for.

[MB and Vikki Beat]

Thoughts Whilst Out Walking

Posted October 21, 2018

Originally written October 2012

FRAN'S WORDS from a few days ago are still with me: "The truest response is letting go …"

Yes … let go of pain, of joy, of aching, of delight … Do not hold on to any of it. Let it rise, have its moment, and go, to be replaced by what arises in its stead … externally and within you. Offer minimal resistance … Let it pass through you, joyously, gratefully …

We cling, we hold on, from fear. Fear of losing what was never ours to begin with. Fear of daring to reach for what is within our grasp.

This moment is all that you will ever own. It is what you have brought into being, it is what you were brought into being to experience, *herenow*. You are the universe's gift to itself in this moment. No other has been granted this gift. Accept it, take it in your hands, examine its shape, colours, textures. Allow it fully into your awareness … And let it go again …

Life is not a lesson, though you can choose to see it as such. Life is not a trial, though you are free to live yours as though it were.

Any gift worth the name comes without strings … you are free to decline it, trample on it, pass it on to another, keep it under lock and key … And so it is with life, with this moment.

[MB]

Acknowledgements

Fran and I would like to thank Sarah Fader and everyone formerly at Eliezer Tristan Publishing for inspiring this collection and publishing the first edition. We are grateful to Kingston Park Publishing for the opportunity to bring our writing to a new and wider audience.

Many of our articles are inspired by conversations with friends. There are too many to mention individually, but we thank you all for your encouragement, wisdom, and caring support. Fran wishes to thank Bob Keyes, Diane Atwood, Donna Betts, and Donna Murphy for being there in so many ways. I'm grateful to Aimee Wilson for encouraging me with humour, creative suggestions, and advice as I prepared this new edition, and to Jen Evans for her gentle support and colour sense. Special thanks to Vikki Beat who contributed to several pieces in this collection.

We are grateful to the many guest writers we've published on our blog, especially mental health blogger and author Aimee Wilson of I'm NOT Disordered, and best-selling author and coach Julie A. Fast. Your passion, authenticity, and determination inspire us and remind us why we do what we do.

Above all, we thank you, our readers. Without you, none of this would mean a thing

About the Authors

Martin Baker graduated in pharmacy in 1983 and completed postgraduate research at King's College London. Despite this academic background, he had little experience of mental illness until a chance encounter online in 2011. His transatlantic relationship with American writer and photographer Fran Houston taught him about living with illness, but more importantly what it means to be a good friend. Despite living three thousand miles away, he is now Fran's primary support and caregiver. Inspired to expand his knowledge and experience, Martin is engaged in the mental health community on both sides of the Atlantic. Certified in Mental Health First Aid and Applied Suicide Intervention Skills Training, he is a member of the National Alliance on Mental Illness, Mind, and Bipolar UK. Martin lives in the north-east of England with his wife and son.

Fran Houston graduated from the University of Tennessee, Knoxville, in 1991, and worked as a successful electrical engineer until she was overtaken by illness. She was diagnosed with major depression in 1994 and with bipolar disorder in 2003. She also has chronic fatigue syndrome (CFS/ME) and fibromyalgia. Inspired by Peaks Island's rich history, Fran interviewed and photographed long-time residents. Publication of *For the Love of Peaks: Island Portraits and Stories, a Collection* in 2010 led to her appearing on Maine Public Broadcasting Network and National Public Radio to discuss her book and the challenges of living with illness. She has been a columnist in the *Island Times*. Her Maine Voices Opinion Editorial appeared in the *Portland Press Herald / Maine Sunday*

Telegram for Mental Health Awareness Week 2015. An open letter to her psychiatrist was published in *The Maine Review*. Fran loves her home town of Portland, Maine, and her many friends who love her dearly.

Their book *High Tide, Low Tide: The Caring Friend's Guide to Bipolar Disorder* was published in 2016. A revised edition by Kingston Park Publishing was published in 2021.

They blog at www.gumonmyshoe.com on mental health and supportive friendships.

No one is too far away to be cared for or to care.

Kingston Park Publishing
kppublishing.co.uk

Kingston Park Publishing